Cool
Parent
101
Fun Things to
Make Your
Kid Say
WOW!

Cool
Parent
101

Fun Things to
Make Your
Kid Say
WOW!

Alecia T. Devantier
and Carol A. Turkington

SOURCEBOOKS, INC.®
NAPERVILLE, ILLINOIS

Published by Sourcebooks, Inc.
P.O. Box 4410, Naperville, Illinois 60567-4410
(630) 961-3900
FAX: (630) 961-2168
www.sourcebooks.com

Library of Congress Cataloging-in-Publication Data
Devantier, Alecia T.
  Cool parent 101 / by Alecia T. Devantier and Carol A. Turkington.
    p. cm.
  ISBN 1-4022-0339-X (alk. paper)
  1. Handicraft. 2. Cookery—Study and teaching (Elementary)—Activity programs. 3. Creative activities and seat work. 4. Parent and child.
I. Title: Cool parent one hundred one. II. Title: Cool parent one hundred and one. III. Turkington, Carol. IV. Title.
TT157 .D48 2004
745.5—dc22
                    2003026308

Printed and bound in the United States of America
BG 10 9 8 7 6 5 4 3 2 1

To Simon—Dreams really do come true.
ATD

Table of Contents

Introduction   xi

Tips for Keeping Your Cool   xiii

Tips for Staying Cool   xv

Cool Parent 101 Curricula...

1. Gifts of Giving   1

2. Ant Habitats   4

3. A Backseat Survival Kit   7

4. Beach in a Jar   10

5. A Bird Tree   12

6. The Box Project   15

7. Brain Busters   17

8. Edible Bread Art   19

9. Casting Animal Tracks   23

10. CD Recycle   25

11. Cinnamon Holiday Ornaments   29

12. Color   31

13. Colorful Crispy Cereal Treats   33

14. Cookie Bowls   35

15. Cool Codes and Secret Ciphers   38

16. Crazy Crayons   41

17. A Crystal Garden   43

18. Cool Cupcake Birthday Candles   46

19. Dinner Around the World 49

20. Homemade Dog Bones 51

21. Door Décor 53

22. Face Paint 56

23. A Family Cookbook 58

24. Family Earth Day 60

25. Fingerprints 62

26. Fizzy Rockets 64

27. Friendship Bracelets 67

28. Funny Feet 70

29. Fuzzy Fleece Blankets 72

30. Games from Around the World 75

31. Garden Stones 78

32. Grandparents 81

33. A "Grocery Store" 84

34. A Growth Chart 86

35. Homemade Gumdrops 88

36. A Holiday All Their Own 90

37. Holiday Crackers 93

38. Your Own House 95

39. Ice Candles 97

40. Indoor Scavenger Hunts 100

41. Invisible Messages 102

42. A Journal and a Journal Jar 104

43. Make-Your-Own Jigsaw Puzzles 108

44. A Little "I Love You" 111

45. Macaroni Ornaments 114

46. Magic Mirrors 116

47. Mail 119

48. Maple Ice Candy 122

49. Marbled Ornaments 125

50. Homemade Marshmallows 127

51. Memory Cards 130

52. A Memory Quilt 133

53. A Mini-Garden 136

54. A Money Can 138

55. Morning Muffins 140

56. No-Bake Cookies 143

57. Painted Leaf Prints 145

58. Homemade Paper 148

59. "Paper" Dolls 152

60. Party Platters 155

61. Peanut Butter Balls 158

62. Piñatas 161

63. Plane Entertainment 164

64. Powdered Drink Mix 166

65. Homemade Pretzels 169

66. Pumpkin Carving 172

67. Puppy Chow for People 175

68. Rainy Days 178

69. A Rain Gauge 180

70. Rain Sticks 182

71. Red, White, and Blue Desserts 185

72. Shrink-Plastic Tags 187

73. Homemade Silly Putty 190

74. Snow Globes 192

75. Snowmen 195

76. Snowy Snowman Mints 198

77. Homemade Soap with a Surprise 200

78. Spray-Painted Shirts 203

79. Stained Glass Candy 206

80. Star Spangled Tees 209

81. Star Treatment 211

82. Make Your Own Stickers 214

83. Stone Soup 216

84. Stories 219

85. Sunshine 222

86. Super Simple Cookies 225

87. Surprise Gift Balls 227

88. Sweet Dreams 229

89. An Old-Fashioned Taffy Pull 232

90. Tangrams—An Ancient Puzzle 235

91. Terrific Timepieces 237

92. Tin Can Night Lights 240

93. Make-Your-Own Toy Train 242

94. Tricky Pictures   244

95. Tumbling Blocks (Jacob's Ladder)   246

96. Make-Your-Own Watercolor Paints   251

97. Winter Warmers   253

98. Woolly Balls   256

99. *Your* Childhood Favorites   259

100. Your *Child's* Memories   262

101. Together Time   264

About the Authors

Introduction

Childhood is a magic time, full of opportunities for parents and children to share magical moments and make magical memories. Some of those moments will be once-in-a-lifetime experiences such as birthday celebrations, special summer family vacations, trips to a theme park, attending a softball game or theater production, and celebrating the holidays.

However, the best magical moments you share with your children—those memories they'll carry with them throughout their lives—are the day-to-day things you share: helping Dad wash the supper dishes, weeding the garden with Mom, playing a game of Go Fish!, or sharing a story with the whole family before bedtime.

One of the best things about the magic found in these everyday events is that they don't cost anything in dollars and cents—just in the time we take to spend with our kids. Our families might not be able to travel to Disney World every year, but we can create a new family favorite cookie recipe, come up with new holiday decorations, or volunteer together for our community. In this way, those magical moments and events in our lives give rise to family traditions.

This book contains a wide range of activities that you can share with your child. Perhaps you'll set up a Bird Tree each winter, or maybe you'll make a new cupcake candle for your child on each birthday. You might add a Red, White, and Blue Dessert to your annual Independence Day picnic, or maybe you could host a Stone

Soup supper each fall. You may want to create a Memory Quilt each year or just a single square to be incorporated into a quilt you build over time. Perhaps you'll build a set of dishes by painting Party Platters several times a year.

Traditions don't need to cost lots of money or take a lot of time. Simply *enjoying* a routine activity can turn it into a tradition that your family can carry on for generations to come. Look what the Pilgrims started when they gathered together some turkeys and vegetables to give thanks in America!

You may discover that some of the activities in the pages that follow will be so magical that you'll repeat them time and time again—and a few new traditions will be born for your family.

Tips for Keeping Your Cool

Nearly any experience has the potential to become a magic moment. Here are some tips to smooth the path for truly magical events.

Read the instructions all the way through first. There is nothing magical about trying to figure out what is going on when you are in the middle of a project. Determine if your child's skills and abilities match the requirements of the project. Otherwise, *you* might end up doing the whole thing.

Collect all the supplies that you'll need before starting a project. Not having the materials or tools needed for each step can ruin a magic moment. For the activities in this book, we assume that you have basic kitchen and crafting supplies on hand. These items are not listed in the materials needed for the project, so before getting started make sure you have everything you'll need.

Try to avoid interruptions when working on a project with your child. If possible, turn off your cell phone and pager, let the answering machine pick up any calls, and turn off the television. If you want some background music, select something classical or soothing. Working together without interruptions will allow you and your child the opportunity to talk, laugh, and perhaps most important, to make a magic memory.

Plan enough time to complete the project. A potentially delightful memory will be fractured if you abruptly stop in the middle of a project to pick up a child from soccer practice or take someone to a Scout meeting. If your schedule doesn't allow for large blocks of time, figure out a way to break the project or activity into two or more sessions.

Change clothes before starting a project. If you plan to do a number of projects, consider investing in a paint shirt or smock. While you're at it, have some good stain remover on hand in case of an accident.

Resist the urge to clean-as-you-go. Unless it's a big spill, or something that will stain if not cleaned up right away, let your child work and create without the worry or interruption of cleaning up at every step along the way. Save the clean-up for when the project is complete and do it together with your child.

Tips for Staying Cool

If you are going to take the time to create terrific memories with your child, why not do all you can to preserve the symbols of those magic moments for a lifetime? It's easier than you might think.

Whenever possible, give your child the best supplies possible with which to create. If your child is like most, you know that it often seems that his or her most creative work is done on a scrap piece of paper, the back of an envelope, or a piece of brittle construction paper. And it's almost always impossible to re-create that work of art with supplies that will stand the test of time. So, work with quality supplies from the beginning, if you can.

Look for ways to make the project permanent. For example, maybe your child learns to carve pumpkins and turns them into works of art. Unfortunately, a carved pumpkin will last only for a few weeks and then end up in the trash can. Foam pumpkins can be found at craft stores, and your child's original work of art can brighten your décor for years.

Frame a few of your child's drawings. If your child enjoys drawing so much that you've accumulated an unmanageable pile of drawings, frame a few and change them out on a weekly or monthly basis. Alternatively, have your child draw the pictures in a spiral-bound scrapbook; you'll be able to keep a tidy, lasting record of your little one's artwork.

Look for other activities that relate to your project. Many of the ideas in this book have a "Stay Cool" component that describes a related activity, book, or movie to share with your child.

Gifts of Giving

One of the most special experiences that a parent can have with a child comes from sharing time and talent with others who may be less fortunate. Parents can help their children learn the great gift of a caring and generous heart. The key is not the amount of money you spend but the effort and emotion that goes into your child's volunteer effort.

Perhaps your family—along with a well-behaved family pet—could visit the residents at a local nursing home. Or maybe your family could "rescue" teddy bears and dolls from local garage sales, clean them up, add new ribbons or clothing, and donate them to a service agency for children in need. If you want to do something close to home, consider spending an afternoon washing outside windows, raking leaves, or doing yard work for an elderly neighbor who needs a little extra help. Even preschoolers can join in by coloring cards or pictures for area shut-ins, nursing-home residents, or hospital patients. Look around your community for ways that you and your child can get involved.

Here are some suggestions for magic moments that you can turn into gifts of giving.

Colorful Crispy Cereal Treats (page 33) are a bake sale favorite. Cook up several batches next time you're called up to donate for a bake sale. Or organize a bake sale and donate the proceeds to a worthy cause.

Make several batches of Crazy Crayons (page 41) and donate them along with a few coloring books to area preschools, hospitals, doctors' offices, or shelters.

Decorate several pairs of Winter Warmers (page 253) mittens to donate to a mitten tree or community service agency that will distribute them to those in need.

Volunteer to plant flowers or pull weeds in a neighbor's yard, or sign up for a community beautification project. Make a special Garden Stone (page 78) to add to your gardening project.

Whip up colorful bars of Surprise Soap (page 200) for the children in your local homeless or women's shelter.

Organize your Scout troop, church group, school class, or neighbors and friends and make Tumbling Blocks (page 246) by the dozens. Donate them to local community service agencies for their holiday care packages for the kids.

Host a Stone Soup (page 216) dinner for your friends, neighbors, or church group. Assign everyone an item to bring, and ask them to bring twice as much as you need for the soup. Donate the extra ingredients to your local food pantry or soup kitchen.

Spend a rainy afternoon creating colorful Stained Glass Candy (page 206) sun catchers. Deliver the sun catchers to a local

nursing or retirement home, the children's ward at the hospital—
or to anyone who could use a little sunshine.

Ant Habitats

If you've ever watched a bunch of kids lying on the ground staring at an anthill, you know the attraction that ants can hold. Capture the interest of your budding entomologists by having youngsters make their own ant habitat! Ants are quiet, low-maintenance pets—no shedding hair! They'll provide plenty of fascination for kids who follow the simple instructions below to make their own ant habitat.

To make an ant habitat, you'll need:

A large glass jar

A soft drink can

Dirt

Ants from the same ant hill

A piece of sponge

A piece of cloth

A rubber band

Black construction paper

Tape

Dry pet food or small pieces of fruit

1. Put the soft drink can into the center of the glass jar. (The can will push the dirt near the outside of the jar, requiring the ants to build where they're more visible.)

2. Fill the glass jar loosely with dirt to the top of the soft drink can.

3. Add ants. (They must be from the same anthill because ants from different colonies will fight.)

4. Place a wet piece of sponge on top of the soft drink can, and keep it moist—but not too wet. Ants will die if they get too much water.

5. Cover the jar with a piece of cloth. Secure the cloth with a rubber band around the mouth of the jar so the ants cannot crawl out.

6. Tape the black paper around the outside of the jar so the ants will tunnel against the dark sides of the jar. It may take about a week for the ants to start building really complex tunnels.

7. Remove the paper for short periods so your curious child can observe the ants' behavior.

Important: You must feed the ants. Place a small amount of food scraps on top of the dirt. Too much food isn't good for ants. Try a few kernels of dry pet food or small pieces of fruit.

Stay cool!

For a fascinating, fun story about ants, check out *Two Bad Ants* by Chris Van Allsburg at your local bookstore or library.

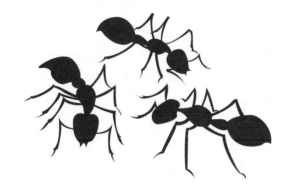

A Backseat Survival Kit

Who doesn't have fond memories of those long family car trips, with everyone singing traveling songs and stopping for picnics along the highway? There's still something to be said for the family road trip, but to make it really special, have something to occupy the kids when they aren't napping or noshing. The Backseat Survival Kit is filled with all kinds of items to occupy the most restless child and keep things amicable between siblings.

Choose one container for a Backseat Survival Kit for each child so there's no squabbling. You can use anything from a plastic grocery store bag to a fancy organizer bag that hangs on the back of the front seat and has zippered pocket and divided sections. Or give each child a plastic box that doubles as a desk for writing or drawing during the trip. Fill it with any of the following items:

A pack of cards

Pens, pencils, crayons, or markers

Small notebooks

A disposable camera

Mad Libs booklets

A small clipboard

A small whiteboard and dry-erase markers

Whiteboard Fun

There's something about a whiteboard that kids just love. Although they come in all sizes, for car trips you'll need to get a small board plus an eraser and plenty of whiteboard markers. (You can use tissues if the eraser gets lost.) The whiteboard gives a modern twist to the old pencil-and-paper classics such as hangman, tic-tac-toe, and more.

For the budding artists in the group, a whiteboard also makes the perfect slate for mobile Pictionary: Mom or Dad writes the subject on a slip of paper and passes it back to the first child, who uses the whiteboard to illustrate the word that the others try to guess. Have the kids take turns drawing to continue the game. If the kids are close enough in age, you can use a timer to see who can guess the word faster.

License Plate Race

The License Plate Race works when traffic exists on both sides of your car. Each child looks out his or her window and chooses either "odd" or "even." The child who chooses "odd" counts only license plates on her side that have an odd number of digits; the "even" child counts license plates on her side that have an even number of digits .

If your kids just don't like numbers, try states. Each child writes down as many different state license plates as possible that pass on "her" side of the car.

Sign of the Alphabet

You and your child can find words beginning with "A" on signs along the road as you drive for a set number of minutes. If you have two or more children, you can assign the players different letters. A different child starts each new game, so everyone gets a chance with the challenging letters. (For younger players you may want to skip the difficult letters.) Alternatively, each child can look for signs out of their own window and race to reach the end of the alphabet first.

For Everyday Trips

Select a few small toys that your child enjoys but hasn't played with for a while and pack them away in a small plastic "boredom bag" that you'll keep with you up front in the car. As kids get bored or fussy, dole them out one or two at a time from the bag. Or stop by a discount store and buy a few small items for the bag that your kids might like.

Beach in a Jar

After you shake the sand from your shoes and the salt from your clothes, you're probably left with a couple of big bags of shells and a lot of sun-filled memories after your beach vacation. Here's a way to recapture some of those magical memories and recycle the kids' treasures into a lasting remembrance of a golden family summer.

To make this beach-in-a-jar scene, you'll need:

Interesting glass jar with lid*

Glass cleaner

Sand from the beach

Small shells of different varieties, pebbles,

small pieces of driftwood

* Note: Different shapes and sizes of jars will give a different "look" to your sea scene. Experiment to find what you like best.

1. Use glass cleaner to remove fingerprints from the inside and outside of the jar.

2. Decide if the jar is going to sit upright or lie on its side.

3. Pour enough sand into the jar to cover the bottom.

4. Drop shells, pebbles, and pieces of driftwood inside the jar.

5. Put the lid on the jar. To rearrange the view, simply rotate or turn the jar gently.

These not only make great holiday gifts for grandparents, but they are nice mementos to keep on your desk to remind you of the summers you spent with your child.

Stay cool!

To make sure these memories aren't forgotten, give your child some paper and have her write a story or poem about her beach experience, or ask him to create some artwork about his favorite beach memories from this vacation. Consider making one or two of the poems, stories, or artwork more permanent by framing and hanging the efforts for everyone to enjoy.

5

A Bird Tree

There's a magical world of feathered and furry inhabitants right outside your window. Pick up a few books to read about who might be stopping by, and then watch to see which animals actually appear. It's also fun to learn the songs of the birds that are native to your area, because you're likely to hear their voices even if you can't see them. Books can tell you what and where your local birds like to eat and where they built their nests. Reading up on the kinds of birds you can expect in your backyard or park will help you prepare a habitat complete with snacks—and be prepared to make friends!

Making a Home

Pine trees make excellent shelters for birds, especially in the winter when most other trees lose their leaves. Decorate an evergreen tree in your yard with edible ornaments. City dwellers can decorate a tree in the courtyard of apartment buildings or create a miniature version on a patio with a potted evergreen. You might also consider installing a window feeder; fill with seed and other goodies for an up-close view of your feathered friends. (This is fun no matter where you live.)

Edible Garland

Thread the end of a long piece of twine or jute through the eye of a large, plastic craft or darning needle. String toasted oats cereal, dried apples, prunes, and large chunks of bread.

Peanut Butter "Cookies"

Spread a thick layer of peanut butter on large unsalted hard pretzels or on plain bagels sliced in half. Create a loop hanger by slipping twine or jute through the hole in the pretzel or bagel and suspend it from the tree.

"Orange" You Hungry?

Cut an orange or grapefruit in half and scrape out the fruit. Using an awl or knitting needle, make three or four equally spaced holes around the top of the orange. Thread one long piece of twine or jute through each hole and tie the ends together. Before you drape the twine over a branch, fill the "fruit bowl" with birdseed.

A Special "Tweet"

Over low heat, melt together 1/2 cup smooth peanut butter and 1/2 cup solid vegetable shortening. Pour the mixture into a large bowl, and let it cool slightly. Stir in birdseed, cornmeal, and dried fruit until you have a thick "dough" that will hold its shape when packed together. When the mixture is cool to the touch, pack it into large pinecones. Wrap a piece of twine or jute around the cone and let it dangle from a tree.

Stay cool!

Use your tree or window feeder to help scientists learn more about the habits and patterns of birds during the winter months (from November through early April) by participating in the Cornell Lab of Ornithology's Project FeederWatch. By keeping track of who visits your feeder, you can help scientists track the movements of birds in the winter and provide important information about trends in distribution and population. For more information about Project FeederWatch, check out the official website at http://birds.cornell.edu/pfw/. Note: There is a $15 fee to participate in the program.

6

The Box Project

If your family is one of the fortunate ones with a warm place to sleep and plenty of food on the table, it can be hard to help your children understand that others are not quite so lucky. One great way to offer friendship and education to a sister family is to join The Box Project.

For nearly forty years, The Box Project has been working to help people trapped in America's worst areas of rural poverty—places where hardworking people try to raise their families on minimum wage, if they can find any job at all. The Box Project matches a Helper Family with a needy Sister Family in an area of rural poverty. (You can request a family with a child near the ages of your own children. Since The Box Project usually has about four hundred families waiting for Helper Families, this isn't too difficult.)

Once you join The Box Project, each month your family sends to your Sister Family a box of supplies filled with gently-used clothes, food, books, pencils, art materials, and so on. Special boxes with new items may be sent on holidays; a gift certificate to their local food store is always appreciated. The two families exchange letters and photos, and with luck, time, and effort, a wonderful friendship can develop. Involve the kids in packing the boxes, planning what goes in them—and perhaps wrapping special holiday box ingredients.

Families who aren't sure they could handle the monthly responsibility of being a Helper Family can join as a Holiday Helper family, being matched to a Sister Family for just one box during the December holiday season. (These matches are made in September.)

You can email the Box Project at info@boxproject.org or visit their website at http://www.boxproject.org or contact them at: PO Box 435, 87 East St., Plainville, CT 06062, 800-268-9928.

Brain Busters

From the time students learn to write and spell, they're taught that every word has to have a vowel, right?

Wrong.

A Saginaw, Michigan, fifth grader is $50 richer after finding a word without a vowel in the online version of the *Oxford English Dictionary*. The reward was paid by elementary teacher Brenda Bell, who challenges her students each year to find a word in the English language without a vowel. It took fifteen years to find a winner, but Bell made good on her word and paid the prize at the rate of $2 per week for twenty-five weeks.

There are lots of fun ways to help your child stretch her brain. Work together and see if you can solve these brain busters.

- There are actually two "Lincolns" on the United States penny. One is the large profile. Can you find the other? *Use a magnifying glass to see the tiny Lincoln sitting inside the Lincoln Memorial.*

- How much dirt is there in a hole three feet wide, four feet long, and two feet deep? *None, there is no dirt in a hole.*

- Which weighs more, a five pound bag of feathers or a five pound bag of rocks? *They weigh the same: five pounds.*

- Name the four days that begin with the letter "T." *Tuesday, Thursday, today, and tomorrow.*

- Some months have thirty-one days, some have thirty. How many months have twenty-eight days? *They all have twenty-eight days.*

- What does a cow drink? *Water; cows give milk, they don't drink it.*

- Can you jump higher than your dining room table? *Of course you can; your dining room table can't jump.*

- What contains twenty-six letters but only has three syllables? *Alphabet.*

- Can you figure out a way to keep your head underwater for two minutes? *It's easier than you think. Fill a glass with water and hold it above your head for two minutes.*

By the way, the word the fifth grade student found was "psst."

8

Edible Bread Art

Flour, salt, and sugar are staples found in most kitchens. But when you mix them together in the proper proportions (along with water and yeast), something magical happens—bread!

For most children, baking bread from scratch is definitely cool. They enjoy mixing the ingredients, watching the dough rise, kneading it, baking it, and finally eating the finished product. Unfortunately, many adults are intimidated by the whole process.

For a fun, easy alternative, make a batch of unleavened bread that doubles as edible art. This is one of those projects where you'll want to measure out your ingredients into separate bowls before you start mixing.

To make these edible works of art, you'll need:

1/4 cup honey

2-1/2 tbsp. vegetable oil

1/2 cup hot tap water

1/2 cup cold water

2 cups whole wheat flour, plus extra flour for spreading
on the countertop
3/4 cup white flour, divided into 1/2 cup and 1/4 cup portions
1/4 tsp. baking powder
1/4 tsp. baking soda
1/4 tsp. salt
Food coloring and cotton swabs or new, unused paintbrushes
(optional)
A small mixing bowl
A large mixing bowl

1. Preheat the oven to 350°F.

2. In a small bowl, mix together the honey, vegetable oil, and hot water. Stir until well mixed. Set aside.

3. In a separate, large bowl, mix together the whole wheat flour, baking powder, baking soda, salt, and 1/2 cup white flour. Mix in the cold water.

4. Slowly add the honey mixture in the small bowl to the large bowl. Mix well.

5. Work the 1/4 cup white flour into the mixture.

6. Lightly cover a clean countertop or breadboard with wheat flour. Turn the dough out of the bowl onto the floured

surface and knead for about five minutes, until you have stiff dough. Lightly add additional flour to the countertop as necessary to keep the dough from sticking.

7. Use this dough to create edible works of art. You can flatten the dough with a rolling pin until it's about a quarter-inch thick. Cut the dough with cookie cutters or make a variety of free-form designs—anything goes! For best results, keep the creations to the thickness of a half inch or less.

8. To add color to the bread, put several drops of food coloring into a small dish and "paint" onto the dough with a cotton swab or small brush. Thin the food coloring with a few drops of water to lighten the colors, or mix colors together. Mix blue and red to make purple, yellow and red to create orange, and blue and yellow to form green.

9. Bake the bread on non-stick cookie sheets in the center of the oven for fifteen to twenty minutes, or until completely cooked. Designs thicker than a half inch may require extra minutes of cooking time.

10. Cool the bread on a rack. Store the uneaten bread in an airtight container in the refrigerator. Cooled bread can be wrapped in food storage bags or plastic wrap and frozen.

Stay cool!

Arrange a tour of a local bread shop or bakery to see how they make bread. If your child is really interested, consider signing the two of you up for a class on bread baking.

9

Casting Animal Tracks

If you've noticed that your family has turned to solitary pursuits like watching TV, playing video games, and surfing the Internet, maybe it's time to look for some cool ideas that the whole family can enjoy. What about heading outdoors for a family hike or just exploring your own backyard? You can look for bird nests, animal habitats, and animal tracks. You can even make plaster casts of the animal footprints that you find!

Here's what you'll need to keep track of these footprints:

A tin can or coffee can large enough to surround an animal track

Non-stick cooking spray

1/2 cup plaster of Paris

Water

A can opener

First, locate some animal tracks with clean features. Look in damp or sandy areas where the soil is soft. Be careful not to change the track imprint or loosen soil from the track. Here's how to make your tracks:

1. Cut both ends from a tin can using your can opener.

2. Place the tin can over the track and press it lightly into the soil to seal it.

3. Mix 1/4 to 1/2 cup plaster of Paris with water until it's about as thick as pancake batter.

4. Coat the inside of the can with spray-on cooking oil.

5. Pour the plaster into the can, covering the track and then filling the can about an inch deep.

6. Let the plaster dry at for least an hour before moving the can. After twenty-four hours, you can remove your cast from the can.

Stay cool!

Sit down with your child and read *Track Finder* by Dorcas Miller, an excellent book about animal tracks of eastern North America. The book will help you figure out what kind of tracks or prints from animals you may discover.

10

CD Recycle

If you have kids, you've probably got a towering pile of old CDs in the corner. With just a little bit of creative flair, your kids can turn them into cool refrigerator or locker magnets, space age coasters, or shiny sun catchers.

CD Magnets

CD magnets are great for the inside of a locker. They are not only decorative, but the shiny CD media doubles as a mirror.

To make this great back-to-school craft, you'll need:

Old music or computer compact discs

Paint markers

Photos, pictures, stickers, or small decorations

White craft glue

Magnets with a sticky side or a magnet sheet

1. Decorate the shiny side of the CD with photos, paint, or any designs you wish.

2. Affix magnets to the back of the CD with the glue.

3. Hang the magnets on the refrigerator or in a locker.

CD Coasters

Make CD coasters for guests at any get-together where coasters will come in handy. You can add each guest's name to the coaster so everyone knows which drink is whose.

To make CD coasters for your next party, you'll need:

2-1/2 inch round stickers

Markers, pens, or colored pencils

Old music or computer compact discs

Clear contact paper or laminating sheets

Paint markers (optional)

1. Draw a design (and add a guest's name if you wish) on each sticker.

2. Apply the decorated sticker to the center of the shiny side of the CD.

3. Cut a round circle that is slightly larger than the sticker out

of clear contact paper (or laminating sheet).

4. Apply the circle of contact paper (or laminating sheet) over the sticker. This prevents the ink on the sticker from smearing if the person's glass sweats.

5. Decorate the outer portion of the disc with paint markers.

CD Sun Catcher

CD sun catchers will reflect a rainbow of colors, inside and out. They are also great in the trees around your garden because they will keep the neighborhood birds from stealing the fruits (or vegetables) of your labor.

For each sun catcher, you'll need:

2 old music or computer compact discs
White craft glue
Paint markers (optional)
Fishing line or ribbon (at least 8 to 12 inches long)

1. If desired, decorate the shiny side of each CD with paint markers.

2. Glue the CDs together, shiny sides out.

3. Tie a fishing line or ribbon through the hole. (The fishing

line will seem to "disappear" and make the CD look like it's floating.)

4. Suspend the fishing line or ribbon on a curtain rod in a window or from a hook in the ceiling.

11

Cinnamon Holiday Ornaments

Whether your family is celebrating Thanksgiving, Christmas, Hanukkah, Kwanzaa, or the Fourth of July, everyone enjoys the down-home spicy smell of cinnamon ornaments. They're so fun and easy, even the youngest members of the family will be able to create their own holiday decorations.

To make these super-easy ornaments, you'll need:

Ground cinnamon

Applesauce

Waxed paper

Cookie cutters

A drinking straw
Assorted ribbon

1. Set aside 1/4 cup of cinnamon to sprinkle on work surface.

2. In a mixing bowl, combine equal parts cinnamon and applesauce until the mix resembles cookie dough.

3. Chill the mixture in the refrigerator for about two hours.

4. On a flat surface, sprinkle some ground cinnamon. Roll out half of the dough to the thickness of a quarter inch. Add more cinnamon as needed to keep the dough from sticking. (Do not use flour!)

5. Cut out various shapes with cookie cutters, and place the ornaments on baking sheets.

6. Before the ornaments dry out, poke a hole through the top of each shape with a straw.

7. Cover the baking sheets with waxed paper and set the shapes aside for several days, until they dry out.

8. When the ornaments are thoroughly dry, tie a ribbon through each hole to form a loop.

12

Color

Very early on, children start to express favorites when it comes to color. Most preschoolers even have a favorite, which usually dominates their artwork. It's amazing that all of the colors in the rainbow can be created from different combinations of red, blue, and yellow. There are lots of fun ways to teach basic color concepts, so why not spend an afternoon making some colorful magic?

Yellow and Blue Make Green

One simple way to "make" colors requires a coffee filter and water-based markers. Working on a piece of cardboard, flatten a coffee filter, and color a thick yellow circle about 1 or 2 inches to the left of the center. To the right of the yellow circle—but not quite touching—color a blue circle. Fold the filter in half three times, creating a pie-wedge shape. Dip the pointed tip into a cup of water and let it sit long enough for the water to soak past the outer edge of the filter. After the filter sits for a couple of minutes, unfold it to reveal the patterns and colors created by mixing the yellow and blue! Try pairing blue and red circles, or red and yellow circles.

For another unique way of creating secondary colors, you'll need a bright flashlight and three small balloons (red, blue, and yellow). Cut the neck off each balloon. To create colorful magic, stretch a balloon tightly over the flashlight lens. Add a second balloon over the top. Take your child into a dark room and turn on the flashlight. Change the balloons to create other colors.

Colorful Art

With just a few ingredients you can create colorful components for your child to use in his artistic creations. In a small zipper-top bag, combine 1 teaspoon of rubbing alcohol and several drops of food coloring, add 1/4 cup macaroni or rice. Mix until the contents are evenly colored. Spread the contents on paper towels. Once dry, they can be glued to artwork or layered in jars. The macaroni can be strung for bracelets or necklaces. Be aware that the colored rice and pasta are *not* edible.

Stay cool!

Colorized photos are very popular and very simple to do at home. Have black and white photos developed or reproduced on matte paper. Use special photo tinting pens to color as desired. Younger children can colorize black and white photocopies with colored pencils or markers.

13

Colorful Crispy Cereal Treats

Marshmallow and rice cereal treats have been a family favorite for more than sixty years. Generations of parents and children have created memories together by making and eating these gooey snacks. Your family can make some new memories with a twist on this family favorite.

Create your treats with traditional holiday colors or make a batch in your favorite team's colors. Try adding cherry drink mix with chocolate chips, lime flavor with cinnamon candies, orange drink with chocolate covered raisins, or just plain grape...inventing new combinations is almost as fun as eating them!

To make these terrific treats, you'll need:

Non-stick cooking spray

1/3 cup margarine

5 cups mini-marshmallows

1 (4-serving size) package flavored gelatin or
1/2 cup pre-sweetened drink mix
6 cups crisp rice cereal
1/2 to 1 cup candy pieces, chocolate chips, raisins, etc. (optional)
Food coloring (optional)

1. Spray a 9 x 13-inch pan with non-stick cooking spray. These treats are sticky, so be sure to spray even non-stick pans well. Set the pan aside.

2. In a large saucepan, melt the butter over low heat. Add the marshmallows and stir until they are melted. For gooier treats, reduce the amount of cereal by 1/2 cup, or add 1/2 cup extra marshmallows.

3. Remove the pan from the heat and mix in the gelatin or drink mix, stirring until it is dissolved. For more intense color, add a few drops of food coloring.

4. Add the cereal and mix thoroughly.

5. If desired, mix in the candy pieces, chocolate chips, raisins, candy pieces, etc.

6. Using a spatula sprayed with non-stick cooking spray, press the mixture into the prepared pan. Allow the mixture to cool, then cut it into squares. Store the squares in an air-tight container at room temperature.

14

Cookie Bowls

Close your eyes and think back to when you were a child...do you remember the smell of just-baked cookies wafting out of the oven, or your mom waiting for you to come home from school with a big glass of milk and a plate of piping-hot chocolate chip cookies? Some of our most favorite moments are intricately linked with kitchen smells: perking coffee, sizzling bacon, baking bread and cookies.

Baking cookies with your own children is a wonderful way to pass along that kitchen tradition. If you're interested in baking something a little different than the same-old typical cookies, consider baking a "cookie bowl." The bowl itself is made of cookie dough! Filled with treats, they make great gifts at holiday time, for shut-ins, or for a party. And if you use refrigerated cookie dough, they're so easy that kids of almost any age can do it.

Here's what you'll need:
1 package of refrigerated sugar cookie dough
Vegetable shortening
Waxed paper

A round cookie cutter or drinking glass
Parchment paper
Aluminum foil
An oven-safe mixing bowl, about 11 inches wide

1. Preheat the oven to 350° F.

2. Roll out refrigerated cookie dough between two sheets of waxed paper to one-inch thickness. Make sure the dough is cold!

3. Cut out round shapes from the dough with a round cookie cutter or a drinking glass.

4. Turn your oven-safe mixing bowl upside-down. Cover it with aluminum foil, and grease the foil. Remember: the bowl must be oven-safe.

5. Place a cookie-dough circle on the now upturned bottom of the bowl. Drape other round circles of dough over the inverted mixing bowl, overlapping and gently pressing the edges of the circles together. Only cover the bowl about halfway down the sides—the dough will rise in the oven! Try to make the dough an even thickness around the out-side of the bowl and a little thicker where the base of the bowl will be.

6. Cut small shapes out of the leftover dough with cookie cutters. Place the shapes on a separate cookie sheet. When baked, you can apply these with frosting to decorate the outside of the cookie bowl.

7. Bake the small shapes for six minutes; bake the cookie bowl for about fifteen minutes, until the edges turn lightly brown. Transfer the shapes and the bowl to a rack and cool.

8. Attach the small shapes to the cookie bowl with frosting.

9. To remove the cookie bowl, carefully lift it from the foil-lined bowl, and gently turn it over.

10. Arrange other cookies or treats in the cookie bowl. Cover loosely with plastic wrap until ready to serve.

Stay cool!

Experiment with other types of oven-proof bowls, loaf pans, or containers to make lots of different kinds of cookie bowls. Pack a cookie bowl with some great cookies and take to a senior-citizen home to share with residents, or drop off a cookie bowl to your local post office workers to enjoy during a busy holiday season.

15

Cool Codes and Secret Ciphers

Kids like to write notes to each other, sharing special secrets or the news of the day. Help them take it one step further by teaching them how to write those messages in code. They'll not only turn into secret agents, they'll strengthen and reinforce their writing and problem-solving skills, too.

Simple Substitution: ABC and 123

Probably the simplest substitution code to teach your child is a "shift code." Write the alphabet A through Z across the top of a piece of paper. Underneath this string of letters, write the alphabet again, only this time offset or shift the letters so that, for example, "A" is beneath "B," "B" is beneath "C," and so on. Coding messages in this way has been done for thousands of years. Even Julius Caesar used this method to send secret messages. The code's key would look like this:

```
A B C D E F G H I J K L M N O P Q R S T U V W X Y Z
z a b c d e f g h i j k l m n o p q r s t u v w x y
```

Using the above code, the phrase "Dear Kate" would become "cdzq jzsd."

This same method can be used with numbers instead of letters. Write out the letters A through Z and then assign the numbers 1 through 26 to the letters.

Random Substitution

Once they've mastered simple substitutions, kids will be ready for the challenge of creating codes at random. To create a random alphabet code, substitute one letter for another with no pattern. Instead of a simple shift, randomly assign one letter for another. You can create a number code in a similar fashion. Once you've mastered these random codes, consider creating a completely random code using the symbols and characters you find on the computer keyboard. You might choose to substitute "@" for "A," "4" for "B," "X" for "C," and so on.

Backwards (But-Not-Quite-Coded) Messages

Children love to send and receive messages written in mirror-image. With a computer and printer, these messages are a snap to create. To make a mirror-image, type up the message in the word processor program of your choice, and when you print, select the "mirror image" option. To read the message, fold the paper just below the bottom of the message, hold the folded edge against a mirror, and read the message by looking at its reflection in the mirror.

Advanced Ciphers

Your budding cryptographers (people who write or solve codes) might enjoy learning Braille, hieroglyphics, Morse code, or American Sign Language as a way to send messages or communicate with friends.

16

Crazy Crayons

To anyone who spends time with young children, it probably comes as no surprise that children aged two through eight years spend an average of twenty-eight minutes each day coloring. By the time those children turn ten, they have worked their way through 730 crayons. That's more than 220 feet of crayons—or about fifty-five second graders lying head-to-toe!

There is something cool about those sticks of paraffin wax and colored pigments. You can almost guarantee that every house with children also has a box or two of old crayon stubs stashed away somewhere. Give those old stubs new life by turning them into "Crazy Crayons."

To make these colorful creations, you'll need:
A non-stick cupcake tin (or foil baking cups)

A baking sheet

Crayon stubs

Kitchen shears or sharp knife (adult use only)

Toothpicks (optional)

1. Remove any paper wrappers from the crayons.

2. An adult should cut or break them into pieces about 1/2 inch or smaller. The smaller the pieces, the easier they melt.

3. Preheat oven to about 200°F.

4. Place enough crayon bits into the wells of the cupcake pan or the foil baking cups to fill them about half full. Use stubs in the same color family, or mix and match a variety of colors.

5. Place the foil cups on the baking sheet. Place the cupcake pan or baking sheet into the preheated oven.

6. Check on them often. Remove the cupcake pan or baking sheet from the oven as soon as the crayons have melted together (about ten to fifteen minutes). Some unmelted chunks are okay. Use a toothpick to swirl the colors together. *Do not melt the crayon bits until they completely liquefy. If melted to a liquid, the wax and the color tend to separate, and the new crayons will not color well.*

7. Let the new crayons cool. To speed up the cooling time, place the cupcake pan or foil cups in the refrigerator.

8. Once the crayons are cool, pop them out of the cupcake pan or peel away the foil wrapper. You'll have big round crayons that are great for little hands and lots of fun for big kids, too!

17

A Crystal Garden

Children are fascinated by watching things grow. If you've ever planted flower or vegetable seeds with a child, you've probably witnessed that fascination firsthand. They check a dozen times or more a day for the first signs of a sprout. And once it appears, the race is on, and your child cheers for every new leaf or tiny growth.

Plants are fun to grow, but why not make some magic by helping your child grow crystals? These non-edible creations grow very quickly. Depending on your growing conditions, you might see crystals in a matter of hours—a definite plus when working with kids!

To grow your own magical crystal garden, you'll need:

A large, shallow glass pan

A thick kitchen sponge or charcoal bricks

1/4 cup laundry bluing (a product used to counteract yellowing of white fabrics)

1/4 cup water

1/4 cup salt

1 tbsp. ammonia

Food coloring

1. Cut the sponge or break the charcoal into large chunks and place them into the pan. Set the pan aside.

2. In a large disposable plastic cup, mix together 1/4 cup water, 1/4 cup bluing, 1/4 cup salt, and 1 tablespoon ammonia. Halve the recipe for small gardens.

3. Carefully pour the mixture over the pieces of sponge or charcoal. The pieces of sponge or charcoal need to be large enough to stick out of the solution. Scoop any mixture that remains in the cup into the pan.

4. Put a few drops of food coloring onto the pieces of sponge or charcoal. For fun, use different colors on each piece.

5. Set the pan in a warm, dry location where it will be undisturbed. Since the solution is toxic, place it out of the reach of curious young children and pets.

When the crystals stop growing, make another mixture of the solution and add it to the garden. Pour the solution into the container at the base of the crystals, not over the top of the crystals. Add additional coloring as desired.

Stay cool!

For more information on crystal formations, along with ideas and instructions for growing other types of crystals, check out Jean Stangl's *Crystals and Crystal Gardens You Can Grow*.

18

Cool Cupcake Birthday Candles

When children are young, birthdays mean presents—and maybe a party. As they get older, kids still anticipate the presents and the party, but they also look forward to the special traditions that have accumulated over the years: breakfast in bed, a balloon bouquet delivered to school, or dinner at a favorite restaurant.

Another birthday tradition most children look forward to is blowing out the candles on the cake. Start a new tradition for your family with a cupcake-shaped candle that looks good enough to eat.

To make one for your child's next birthday celebration, you'll need:

Newspaper

A cupcake pan

Foil baking cups

A double boiler

(substitute a large saucepan and a large can, like a coffee can,
for the double boiler)
1/4 lb. paraffin wax for each candle
A sharp knife (adult use only)
Birthday candles
Crayon stubs
An empty plastic jar with lid, washed and dried
Plastic knives and/or spoons
Glitter (optional)

1. Cover the work area and floor with newspaper in case of spills.

2. Put *two* foil cups, stacked, into the cupcake pan for each candle to be made. Set the pan aside.

3. Chop the paraffin wax into 1-inch chunks using a sharp knife.

4. Melt the wax over low heat in the top of a double boiler. If making a colored candle, stir in a piece of crayon stub as the wax melts. Wax should not be melted over direct heat or in a microwave.

5. Carefully spoon the melted wax into the foil cups until they are nearly full. There should be wax left in the double boiler.

6. When the wax has set up, but is still soft, insert the bottom inch of a birthday candle into the center of each foil cup. Hold the birthday candle in place for a minute until it's set. Allow the contents of the foil cup to cool completely.

7. Melt the paraffin wax that remained in the double boiler, adding a piece of crayon for color.

8. Allow the wax to cool slightly until a thin film forms on top. Pour the wax into the jar and screw the lid on tightly.

9. Shake vigorously until no liquid wax remains.

10. Use a plastic knife or spoon to apply the wax "frosting" to the candle. If desired, sprinkle with glitter. Let the cupcake candle harden.

11. Remove and discard the outer foil cup.

19

Dinner Around the World

Letting kids help in the kitchen is a great way to teach responsibility while sharing time together. Get the whole family involved by choosing one night a week to have a "Theme Dinner" featuring another country's cuisine and decoration.

Start by writing names of as many countries as possible on slips of paper. Draw one each week to choose the country you'll be focusing on. Everyone can get together to plan simple decorations linked to that country. Older kids can even do some research and choose their own type of food to make. For example, if you pick "France," the menu might include French onion soup, a loaf of crusty French bread from the bakery, a big salad, and crêpes suzette for dessert. Younger kids can join in by coloring white paper napkins in the colors of the French flag (strips of white, blue, and red). Borrow a recording of French music from the library, don berets, and enjoy the meal. During dinner, everyone around the table can offer an interesting fact about France that they've looked up during the week.

Stay cool!

Talk with your children about hunger around the world, and consider how you might help with donations to programs such as the United Nations World Food Programme, where a donation of $34 feeds a child for an entire school year. (U.S. Friends of the WFP, PO Box 11856, Washington, D.C. 20008; or visit their website at www.wfp.org)

20

Homemade Dog Bones

Kids of all ages love homemade treats—not just eating them, but making them as well. Imagine the fun your child would have creating homemade treats for his favorite four-legged family member. Even if you don't have a dog at home, you can bake up a batch or two of some Homemade Dog Bones and share them with your friends' dogs. You could also stop by your local Humane Society or animal rescue group to donate some of your homemade doggie treats. Keep in mind that many people donate to charitable organizations during the holidays, so try to make your donation during a slow time. If possible, spend some time playing with the pups when you deliver the biscuits.

To make these terrific treats for your canine companion, you'll need:

2 cups whole wheat flour

1/4 cup dry milk

3/4 cup chicken or beef broth
(or 2 bouillon cubes dissolved in 3/4 cup hot water)
1 egg, slightly beaten
1/4 cup vegetable oil

1. Preheat the oven to 300°F.

2. Mix the ingredients together until well blended. If the dough is sticky, add a little more flour.

3. On a floured surface, roll out the dough to 1/4-inch thickness. Use large cookie cutters to cut out a variety of shapes.

4. Bake the cookies on an ungreased cookie sheet for 35 to 45 minutes. They should be lightly brown and crunchy, but not burned.

5. Remove to a cooling rack until completely cool. Store them refrigerated in an airtight container.

Unlike store-bought dog bones and treats, this homemade version does not have any preservatives. The treats should be consumed or discarded within a few days.

21

Door Décor

When it comes to decorating your child's room, why should all the fun be limited to the inside of the room? Let your child announce to the world that this is the entrance to his own magical space by letting him decorate the door to his room with fun and simple foam decorations. If your children share a room, make sure to give each one equal space. And, if there are younger siblings toddling about, be sure that the decorations are kept high enough so that little hands won't be able to pull them off.

To help your child create his own personal door décor, you'll need:

Craft foam

Permanent markers

Small, flat buttons

Foam cutouts

Glitter

A piece of paper with your child's name traced or printed on it in very large block letters

Photos of friends, pets, and other favorite things

Glue

Scissors

Decorative-edge scissors (optional)

Cookie cutters (optional)

Removable adhesive

1. Cut out the letters of the name from the paper pattern.

2. Trace the letters onto pieces of craft foam. You can use one color or a variety of different colors. Cut the letters out.

3. Arrange and glue the letters onto a larger piece of foam. When the glue is dry, cut around the letters, making a nameplate for the door.

4. Use permanent markers to add highlights to the letters. Glue on buttons, small foam cutouts, or add glitter to the nameplate.

5. Use additional pieces of foam to create more decorations. Cookie cutters can be used to make great patterns. Embellish with markers, buttons, cutouts, glitter, and more.

6. Make small foam frames for favorite photos. This can be as simple as using decorative-edge scissors to cut a square or

rectangle from the foam and gluing the picture in the center. Don't forget to decorate the frames.

7. When all of the decorations are dry, use removable adhesive to attach them to the door.

22

Face Paint

Your child can take on all sorts of different personalities with just a few dabs of fanciful face paint such as a scowling lion, a mischievous mouse, or a funny clown. If the kids are stuck at home and you're all out of store-bought face paint, don't despair! Here's an easy way to mix up a batch of homemade paint that works just as well.

You'll need:
1 tsp. cornstarch
1/2 tsp. water
1/2 tsp. cold cream
Food coloring
An airtight container
Small paintbrushes

1. Stir together the starch and cold cream until well blended.

2. Add the water and stir.

3. Add the food coloring and stir.

4. Paint designs onto a child's face or let the older kids paint on themselves or each other using a small paintbrush. Face paint can be removed with soap and water.

If you've got larger areas to cover (let's say your child wants to go to a costume party as the Tin Man or the Great Pumpkin...) you can whip up a batch of face paint for all-over painting, using:

1 tbsp. solid shortening
2 tbsp. cornstarch
Food coloring
An airtight container

1. Mix shortening and starch together until smooth.

2. Add food coloring.

3. Use a small cosmetic sponge to apply the paint.

4. The paint can be removed with soap and water.

5. Store the left over concoction in an airtight container.

23

A Family Cookbook

So many good memories are related to good food! Favorite recipes, and the smells and flavors associated with them, seem to help us remember our favorite people and good times.

Today's family get-togethers and the meals shared around the dining room table will be tomorrow's memories for your kids. You can start today to keep a record of some of these favorite recipes—and the moments you share—in a family cookbook. One day, in the hands of your great-great-grandchild, it may become a cherished family heirloom.

Begin with any 2-inch binder or photo album, and insert several packages of three-hole paper and yellow dividers. You can divide the book into sections: by type of food (soups, appetizers, main course), by holiday, or by date.

Ask each member of the family to choose some favorite family recipes to go into the book. Each person can write a favorite recipe onto a page and decorate it if they wish. Encourage each person to write comments on the recipe page. The next time you serve a meal that the family enjoys, add it to the book.

If your book is arranged by date, you can enter the recipe and memories for each special family meal as it occurs. Record holidays, festive parties, or dinners with special guests, plus each family member's special birthday meal. Be sure to describe special family traditions that occur on those dates, too. As the years go by, you'll all be able to look back "through the years" and recount many of your special occasions. Several generations from now, it will serve as a real window into what life was like early in the twenty-first century.

24

Family Earth Day

Many families hope to teach their children ways to improve life and behave responsibly toward our beautiful, but troubled, planet. With this special Earth Day activity, you can combine some family time with practical activism. First, you'll spend some time indoors learning about your family's garbage habits. Next, you'll head out-doors to do something constructive for the environment. Everyone from the youngest child to the oldest teenager can relate to some-thing in this activity.

To begin, give each family member a pair of plastic gloves and send each one to a different room to go through wastebaskets, gathering nonedible, uncontaminated items and placing them in plastic bags. Once everyone has gathered trash items, meet back in the living room. Spread out newspapers on the floor and dump the bags in a pile. Now have your family close their eyes and choose something from the pile. Have everyone look at the item and ask:

1. What is it?
2. Who used it?

3. How could this have been used again so we wouldn't want to toss it?

After you've looked at your own garbage habits, grab a garbage bag for each family member and go out into your community to rid your neighborhood of litter. Start with your own yard and then fan out in the neighborhood. Pick up any bottles and cans, papers or trash you find. If you live in the city and you're uncomfortable picking up trash along busy roads, head to your local park to pick up trash there.

Stay cool!

To find more earth-friendly family activities to do together, check out this book: *Celebrating the Great Mother* by Cait Johnson and Maura D. Shaw. Or think about making a Roots and Shoots project. Check out this program (sponsored by the Jane Goodall Institute) at http://www.janegoodall.org/rs.

25

Fingerprints

From the tops of their heads to the bottoms of their feet, all children are unique. There's one unique feature that each child is born with that he'll carry with him for the rest of his life: his fingerprints. Even identical twins have different fingerprints. Your child can use those one-of-a-kind fingerprints to make some artistic creations that are literally like no one else's.

Getting started: Using nontoxic, washable stamp pads in a variety of colors, practice making thumb and fingerprints in all sorts of shapes and sizes. Let the prints dry before adding any embellishments.

Borders and designs: Use fingerprints in a variety of colors to create a kaleidoscopic design, or simply stamp fingerprints around the border of a store-bought or computer-generated card.

Ladybugs: Use a black marker to add spots, legs, a head, and antennas to a red thumbprint.

Spiders: Start with a thumbprint in your favorite color and use a marker to add a face, eight legs, and a web.

Caterpillars: Make a chain of round fingerprints in the color or colors of your choice. Add a face, a pair of antennae, and feet (two per print).

Snowmen: Stack up a small, medium, and large fingerprint, and use markers to add your favorite snowman accessories (eyes, nose, mouth, buttons, scarf, hat, arms).

Flowers: Stamp a round print for the center of the flower. Make round or oval prints in a different color around the center for petals. Add a stem and leaves with a marker.

Stay cool!

For more ideas of fun things you can create with your fingerprints, check out *Ed Emberley's Great Thumbprint Drawing Book*. When the creating is done, use shaving cream instead of soap as an effective, fun way to clean up inky fingers.

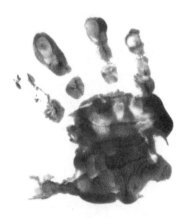

26

Fizzy Rockets

Lots of older kids enjoy building and flying rockets in their backyard, but such toys are far too sophisticated for younger kids. Yet the magic of space flight, exploring other worlds, and alien hunting often captures the attention of much younger children. Here's a fun project appropriate for the younger crowd interested in seeing how rockets work.

You'll need:

A film canister with snap-on lid
A toilet paper roll (double roll size preferred)
Construction paper
Clear tape
Markers, crayons, or paints
Stickers (optional)
Alka-Seltzer tablets
Water in a container
Eye protection

1. Cut straight up the side of the toilet paper roll.

2. Insert the film canister at one end, making sure the end with the lid sticks out about 1/8 inch.

3. Tape along one edge of the toilet paper roll onto the film canister.

4. Roll the toilet paper roll around the canister and tape tightly into place. The canister lid will be the bottom of the rocket.

5. Cut a large pie-wedge shape out of construction paper.

6. Roll the shape into a cone and insert the cone into the open end of the toilet paper tube, with the pointed end of the cone sticking out. Tape the cone in place.

7. Decorate your rocket with markers, stickers, crayons, or paints.

8. Cut 4 squares out of construction paper. Fold the square diagonally. Tape the right-angled edge of the fold against the base of the rocket to make "fins."

9. Go outdoors with the rocket, water, Alka-Seltzer tablets, and eye protection.

10. Put on your eye protection. Turn the rocket upside down, remove the lid from the canister, and fill one-quarter full with water.

11. Drop in a tablet and immediately replace the lid and set the rocket upright on the ground. Stand back! Experiment with the number of tablets to see if the rocket will travel higher.

Stay cool!

Topics of space exploration and the universe makes for wonderful dinner table conversation. Older kids might enjoy reading *Rocket Boys: A Memoir* by Homer Hickam. For the younger ones, read together a book like *Roaring Rockets* by Tony Mitton. Hand out paper and crayons and encourage your child to design the wackiest planet, space alien, or rocket ship.

27

Friendship Bracelets

Finding a new best friend with whom your child can share her joys, sorrows, and deepest secrets is very cool. For a lot of children, the discovery is usually celebrated with the exchange of small trinkets. With a few inexpensive supplies and a couple of hours of her time, your child can make a friendship bracelet to present to her best friend.

To help your child make this special token of friendship, you'll need:

Embroidery floss or pearl cotton (size 3 or 5)

A clipboard or safety pin

Beads (optional)

1. Cut six to eight pieces of floss or pearl cotton to 3 ft. long.

(Use different colors for each strand of floss if your child is a beginner.)

2. Align one end of all of the strands and knot them together about 3 to 4 inches from one end.

3. Place the knotted end of the strands under the clip of the clipboard, with the knot nudging against the outside of the clip. Or run the safety pin through the knot and attach it to your child's jeans, right at the knee.

4. Separate the dangling strands.

5. Start with the strand on the left (call this strand #1). Pass this strand over and around the strand to its right (call this strand #2). Then stick the end of strand #1 through the newly-created loop and pull until snug. This is called a "half hitch" knot. Continuing with strand #1, tie a half hitch knot around strand #3, and so on, until you've used strand #1 to tie a half hitch knot around each of your strands. You can work in beads as desired.

6. Strand #2 will have become the left-edge of your work. Repeat the process of tying a half hitch knot around each of the remaining strands.

7. Continue with the left-most strand to tie half hitches around each of the other strands.

8. Work in this fashion until the bracelet is long enough. Tie all the strands together with a pretzel or overhand knot and trim any excess.

Alternating Half Hitch Bracelet

Using two colors of floss or pearl cotton, cut two strands of each color to 3 ft. long. Working with two strands at a time, tie a half hitch knot around the other two strands. Make a half hitch around the other two using the two that were first tied around. Repeat this pattern until the bracelet is the desired length, working in beads if desired. Finish with an overhand knot and trim the excess.

Stay cool!

Use your child's favorite colors to make a special friendship bracelet from you to him. It will serve as a reminder of your love when he is at a friend's house for the night or away for a week at camp, while you are gone on a business trip, or just during the day when you are apart.

28

Funny Feet

This great back-to-school project will have your child showing off her style in a rather unusual way. Using all her favorite colors, she'll love creating a pair of shoes that are guaranteed to be a hit. And they're so fun you'll probably want a pair for yourself.

To make some fun, fashionable footwear, you'll need:

White canvas tennis shoes

A pencil

Brushable fabric paint, or acrylic craft paint and textile/fabric medium

Dimensional fabric/craft paint (puff paint)

Fabric markers and/or permanent markers

Fabric protector spray

1. Remove the laces from the shoes and stuff the shoes with plastic grocery bags.

2. Lightly sketch a design or guidelines with a pencil on the shoes.

3. Mix acrylic paint with textile/fabric medium according to the manufacturer's directions to prevent stiff, peeling paint.

4. Paint the shoes following the sketched design.

5. Heat-set the paint according to the manufacturer's instructions as necessary.

6. Use the markers and dimensional paints to add your finishing touches. To help the dimensional paint adhere to the canvas, drag a straight pin through the dimensional paint along the surface of the shoe.

7. Let the paint dry for 24 to 48 hours, then spray the shoes with a coat of fabric protector spray.

Finishing Touches

Before lacing the shoes, use a permanent marker to add a splash of color to the laces as well. Draw dots, zigzags, a dashed line down the center, or even letters and numbers. Add small plastic beads, buttons, and charms along the laces as you thread them through the eyelets.

Stay cool!

Coordinate a shoes and socks drive with your school class, Scout troop, or church youth group. Donate the footwear locally, or send it to orphanages around the world.

29

Fuzzy Fleece Blankets

Lots of toddlers have security blankets. Sometimes Mom or Dad has a hard time separating child from blanket for a simple trip to the wash! These blankets are far more than just something familiar and comfortable to curl up with at night. To their owner, these blankets are magic. No matter how ragged and worn, these pieces of fabric, fleece, or knitting have the ability to ward off monsters and things that go bump in the night. They're great for hiding under during a thunderstorm. And when paired with a table, they become a major component in creating a really cool hideout. But "security" blankets aren't just for toddlers, "big" kids (even moms and dads, grandmas and grandpas) love a special, warm blanket to curl up with on a cold or rainy night.

For a child, having a personal "blankie" is cool, but so is being able to help Mom or Dad make a special blanket just for her. For kids too young to help make their own blankets, take a trip to the fabric store and let them select the fabric in their favorite colors. Older children might enjoy making blankets for younger siblings, cousins, or friends.

You can even work together as a family to create blankets for children in need around your community, such as victims of house fires or children whose families are homeless.

To make fuzzy fleece blankets with, or for, the special kids in your life, you'll need:

1-1/2 yards fleece fabric

Sharp scissors (adult use only)

1. Wash the fabric with a mild detergent and tumble dry on low.

2. Cut the fleece into a rectangle approximately 3 x 4 ft. and cut a 4-inch square out of each corner. Fleece is thick material, which might be difficult for a young child to cut.

3. Cut fringe strips on all four sides of the blanket, 4 inches long and 1 inch wide. Try to keep them as uniform as possible. For an extra little touch, use pinking shears to cut the fringe.

4. Tie a knot in each piece of fringe where it meets the blanket.

For an extra-heavy blanket, cut and fringe two pieces of fleece identically. Tie the fringe together in pairs, with one strip from each piece of fleece.

Stay cool!

Make several blankets using fabric with bright, cheerful prints and donate them to Project Linus, a 100% volunteer, nonprofit organization that makes blankets for children who are seriously ill or traumatized. For more information, or to find a chapter in your area, check out http://www.projectlinus.org.

30

Games from Around the World

Many families have found that a weekly family game night is a wonderful way to have some special time together. While any game works fine, it can be fun to think about how children in other parts of the world play games. Jump rope, marbles, and tag—all of these games originated in Europe and Asia many hundreds of years ago. With the following game, you'll have the fun of making the game board, and then playing on it.

To make your own version of the African game Mancala, you'll need:

A cardboard egg carton

2 tuna cans, washed, rinsed, and dried

Acrylic craft paint and paintbrush

48 marbles, very small rocks, beads, or beans

1. Paint the egg carton in the color desired.

2. Paint the tuna cans on the outside. (If you paint the inside, the paint will chip off as you play the game.)

3. Paint designs on the side of the egg carton and tuna cans if you wish.

The object of the game: *Collect as many of your opponent's marbles as you can before he clears his side of the egg carton of all its marbles.*

Set up the game: Place the egg carton between the two players. The cups closest to each player are that player's side. Each player places a tuna can at the end of the egg carton and puts four marbles in each of the six cups on his side.

Playing the game: Choose a player to go first. The first player chooses any one of his cups and picks up all the marbles in that cup. Then he drops one marble in the first cup to the right of the original cup, a second marble in the cup next to that, and so on, until the four marbles are gone. If he reaches the end of his side, he drops one marble in his tuna can and continues around to his opponent's side of the egg carton. He does not drop a marble in his opponent's tuna can.

If the player drops his last marble on his side of the carton in an empty cup, he "captures" all of the marbles in his opponent's cup directly across from that cup. All captured marbles, plus the capturing marble, gets put in the player's tuna can.

Winning the game: The game ends when one player runs out of marbles on his side of the egg carton. When the game ends, the other player gets to take all his marbles from his side of the egg carton and place them in his own tuna can. Whoever has the most marbles in his or her own can wins!

31

Garden Stones

If there is one universal feeling parents have about children, it's that they grow up far too fast. When you hold an infant, it's hard to remember that your children were ever that small. It seems like they grow up overnight—from training wheels to a driver's license in the blink of an eye. You can help your child create permanent imprints of his tiny hands and feet in concrete garden stones. By adding a new set each year, you can watch your child grow up alongside the flowers and vegetables.

You'll need:

Stepping stone mold (available at craft stores), or disposable cake pan (9 x 9-inch square or 9-inch round), or disposable plant tray

Non-stick cooking spray

Dust masks and rubber or latex gloves (optional)

Concrete mix (regular or quick-set)

Disposable bucket

Paint stick

Small trowel or putty knife

1/4-inch dowel or stick

Small, durable, weatherproof objects like marbles, river rocks, glass globs, buttons, coins, charms, beads, ceramic tiles, small toys, etc.

Indoor/outdoor paint designed for use on concrete and stone

Brushes or sponges (optional)

1. Spray the mold with non-stick cooking spray. Set the mold aside.

2. Mix a batch of concrete, following the instructions on the bag. You'll need enough concrete to fill the mold 2 inches deep. (Consider wearing face masks, gloves, and protective eyewear when working with the concrete mix as it can cause skin irritation and respiratory problems.)

3. Pour the concrete into the mold. Smooth the surface with a trowel or putty knife. If using quick-set concrete, you'll need to work fairly rapidly to get steps 4 and 5 finished before the surface hardens.

4. When the concrete is set enough to make a mark that holds its shape, have your child make hand or footprints in the mold.

5. Give your child a stick or dowel to write names and dates. Smooth over any mistakes with a putty knife.

6. Now let your child decorate the stone with small items. Embed the items deep enough so that they will be secure when the stone dries.

7. Let the stone dry for 24 hours before removing it from the mold.

8. Let the stone dry an additional 48 hours before your child paints it. Follow manufacturer's instructions for sealing painted areas, if necessary.

9. Place the completed stone in the garden, or use several to create a path.

Another Option

Alternatively, you can simply paint the design of your choice onto store-bought stepping stones or pavers. Using white indoor/outdoor paint, let your child paint one or two layers of base coat on the pavers. When the white is dry, use a variety of colors to decorate the stones.

If you don't have a garden or backyard to decorate with these spectacular stones, consider organizing a school, church, or Scout group, and making stones to place in a local schoolyard or park. After finishing up the stones, kids can make a miniature version (4 x 4 inches to 6 x 6 inches by about 1 inch thick) to take home as a reminder of the stones they made and donated. These smaller stones make great trivets, and maybe someday will become the cornerstone in the child's garden.

32

Grandparents

Grandparents' Day is celebrated on the first Sunday after Labor Day (in September). The idea began in 1970, when Marian Lucille Herndon McQuade from West Virginia started a campaign to designate a special day to celebrate grandparents. Eight years later, the proclamation was signed into law by President Jimmy Carter.

Most grandparents don't get to see enough of their grandchildren. Your children can make this simple picture frame as a memento for their grandparents on their special day.

You'll need:
A photo to frame

Foam board a few inches larger than the photo

A piece of card stock or thin cardboard

A hole puncher

Scissors

White craft glue or glue stick

Thin ribbon or yarn

Fabric paint, foam cutouts, sequins, buttons, yarn, ribbon, feathers (optional)

1. Decide on the shape you'd like your frame to be: oval, star-shaped, zigzagged.

2. Draw the shape on a piece of foam. The shape should be at least 1 inch larger than the photo on all sides.

3. Cut out the design from the foam.

4. Cut a hole in the inside of the foam to let the photo show through. This hole can be any shape you like. It must be smaller than the photo, but big enough to show the important parts of the photograph.

5. Center your picture in the frame and glue it in place.

6. Cut a thick piece of paper for the back of the frame. The paper backing should be slightly bigger than your picture but smaller than the frame. Glue it to the back of the frame.

7. Punch a hole towards the top of the frame with the hole punch.

8. Decorate the frame with foam cutouts, yarn, buttons, feathers, ribbon, fabric paint, or sequins.

9. Tie a thin ribbon (about 6 inches long) through the punched hole to use for hanging the frame.

Stay cool!

The next time your kids go over to Grandma's, send along a tape recorder. Have the kids interview their grandparents about what life was like long ago.

33

A "Grocery Store"

In the old days, every rural village had a country store where the locals gathered around a potbellied stove to play checkers and gossip. General stores sold not just food, but meat, toys, clothing—just about everything from fishing rods to flypaper.

Sadly, most general stores have faded away, but kids still love the idea of "playing store." And you don't need a lot of expensive, store-bought "toy" food to set up a grocery store in your house.

You'll need:
Empty food boxes and containers
Glue
Paper bags
Play money
A real or toy cash register

For the next few weeks, save all of your empty boxes, cans, and bottles. You can glue down the flaps to make cereal boxes, dog food containers, and other boxes look unopened. Wash and dry jars of all sizes and shapes. If you like, you can add clothes, shoes, and toys as "stock" for an "old-time general store."

Paper bags, real or play money, and an old cash register add to the fun.

To set up the store, gather some clean cardboard boxes of various sizes and arrange in a corner of a room. Display items (adding price tags is fun!).

Have one child be the "shopper" and another be the "grocer." This is also a great way of teaching math skills as the shopper uses her "money" to buy certain goods and the grocer has to make change.

Stay cool!

Although general stores are no longer a common sight in this country, a few can still be found in rural areas. Consider taking a family weekend visit to the country and see if you can discover a real old-time general store.

34

A Growth Chart

Kids grow so fast it's hard to fathom how quickly they're growing up. One fun way to chart the passage of time is to create a growth chart for each child in the family.

To make one for your child, you'll need:

Felt or fabric, 4 or 5 ft. long
2 twigs or wooden dowels cut to the width of the fabric
Pieces of colored felt or craft foam
Fabric paint or fabric markers
Measuring tape or ruler
Ribbon
Current photo of your child
Sharp scissors
White craft glue (or glue gun and glue sticks)

1. Cut the fabric or felt to the desired width.

2. Draw designs or trace around simple pictures onto assorted

pieces of fabric or craft foam.

3. Cut out picture frames from pieces of foam or felt; this is where yearly photos of your child will go.

4. Lay out your decorations and picture frames on the large piece of fabric so you can get an idea of how the design will look.

5. Use a tape measure or ruler to mark off measurements from the bottom of the large piece of fabric to the top. Use fabric markers or paint to make the marks. Remember to leave room so you can write in your child's age each time you measure.

6. Glue decorative ribbon or strips of fabric on either side of the large piece of fabric to hide any fraying edges or rough cuts.

7. Use fabric glue or hot glue to affix all decorations, photos, and photo frames to the chart.

8. Roll the top edge of the chart around a twig or wooden dowel and glue it securely in place. Do the same for the bottom edge.

9. Knot a length of ribbon on the top edge's dowel to hang the chart. Start measuring!

35

Homemade Gumdrops

With their fun colors, delicious flavors, and sugar sparkle, it's easy to see why gumdrops are a childhood favorite. You and your child can make these fun chewies in your favorite flavors in your kitchen. For a twist, make orange-flavored gumdrops colored green, or cherry-flavored colored blue. These treats take a long time from start to finish because of the setup and drying time, so plan accordingly before starting this project.

To make homemade gumdrops, you'll need:

1 cup water, divided into 1/3 cup and 1/2 cup

2 envelopes unflavored gelatin

1-1/2 cup sugar, divided into 1 cup and 1/2 cup

Peppermint flavor oil, or other flavor of your choice

Food coloring

1. Spray an 8 x 8-inch pan with non-stick spray. Set the pan aside.

2. Measure 1/3 cup water into a small bowl. Sprinkle both packets of gelatin over the water. Set the bowl aside and let it stand at least five minutes.

3. In a saucepan, mix together the sugar and 1/2 cup water. Cook over medium heat, stirring constantly, until the mixture boils.

4. Reduce the heat to low and stir in the gelatin mixture. Simmer for five minutes, stirring occasionally.

5. Remove from the heat and stir in 1/4 to 1/2 teaspoon flavored oil. Add several drops of color.

6. Pour the mixture into the prepared pan. Refrigerate for three hours. While the mixture chills, pour 1/2 cup sugar into a food storage bag and set aside.

7. After three hours, use a spatula or butter knife to loosen the edges of the mixture, and turn the mixture onto a cutting board. Cut into 1/2- to 1-inch cubes.

8. Put the cubes into the bag with the sugar, several at a time. Gently shake until all the surfaces are covered. Let the cubes air-dry for three to four hours, turning occasionally, until the sides are all completely dry. Store in an airtight container.

36

A Holiday All Their Own

From Fish Amnesty Day on September 22 to National Lawn Mower Tune-Up Month in March, you can find a special "day" or "month" for just about everyone's favorite activity. If your child had the power to declare a national holiday, what would she celebrate? Maybe her favorite food (National Pizza and Popcorn Night), favorite color (Everyone Must Wear Blue Day), or maybe she would make a personal statement (National No-Homework Week).

While your child can't proclaim a national holiday—at least not yet—why not let her start on a smaller scale by establishing a holiday all her own to celebrate? Before the celebrating can start, your child will need to decide *what* to celebrate. Maybe it will be a favorite food, color, animal, or literary work. Since it's your child's holiday, let her be the one to make the decision, no matter how silly it may seem to you. If the idea isn't appropriate (No-Homework Night, for example), help your child make another choice with some constructive ideas.

Once the theme has been selected, you'll need to select a date to do the celebrating. If you are planning a large celebration with family or friends, make sure you allow ample time for planning and preparation. If you'll be recognizing the event with only your immediate family, you probably won't need as much time to get everything together. If possible, pick a date that is somehow related to the theme. For example, if your child wants to celebrate "*Little House on the Prairie* Day," consider celebrating on February 7, the birthday of author Laura Ingalls Wilder. Or if it's going to be "Butterscotch Pudding Fest" at your house, celebrate on September 19, National Butterscotch Pudding Day.

While it's extra fun to relate the date to something significant, it's not required. The most important thing to keep in mind when selecting a date is your family's schedule. Parents really don't need one more thing added to an already busy week, so schedule the holiday for a time that's convenient. Whatever date you pick, mark it on everyone's calendar well in advance and *stick to it*. Postpone it only in case of an emergency.

Exactly "what you do" or how you celebrate your child's holiday will depend on several factors, but one of the most important is your child's age. A younger child might be happy with an extra scoop of ice cream for dessert to celebrate "Chocolate Chip Cookie Dough Ice Cream Day." Or maybe a bowl of tomato soup with fish crackers followed by an evening watching *Free Willy* with the entire family on "Whale Day." Older kids, who may want more elaborate celebrations, can take more of a role in planning, preparing, and organizing their holiday.

When planning the holiday, brainstorm with your child. Between the two of you, and a little help from the library and the Internet, you should be able to come up with myriad activities for his or her holiday: games; crafts; theme-related stories, songs, and poems; even recipes to round out your holiday with a theme-appropriate feast. Whatever you plan, keep it fun, simple, and low-key. The purpose of the holiday is fun, not stress.

Every celebration needs a special T-shirt to commemorate the event. Even the youngest child can design a logo for the holiday; toddlers can color theme-related clip art enlarged or reduced to the necessary size, and older kids can create their own original artwork with the name of the celebration and the date. When the logo is complete, have a copy shop reverse the image and print it onto iron-on transfer paper so you can make personalized T-shirts for the event.

Stay cool!

Stick with your child's "original" holiday as long as the theme remains one of your child's favorites. Who knows? Maybe twenty-five years from now you'll still be celebrating "Blue Day" on the second Saturday in September, complete with blue jeans and blue logo shirts, blue milk on the breakfast cereal, sandwiches on homemade blue (colored) bread for lunch, and blueberry pie for dessert—served on blue plates (of course).

37

Holiday Crackers

"Christmas crackers," colorful tubes filled with toys, a puzzle, and a paper hat are an old British tradition, but they're fun for any holiday occasion. Make your own holiday crackers and turn them into a family tradition to be enjoyed at a yearly holiday celebration!

To make holiday crackers, you'll need:

A toilet paper roll

Crepe paper or gift wrap

Ribbon

Stickers

Cracker filling such as small candies, confetti (kids can make their own confetti by punching holes from different colored paper and gift wrap), little toys, or a "treasure map."

1. Cut a piece of crepe paper or gift wrap 10 x 10 inches square.

2. Wrap the paper around the toilet paper roll, leaving an even amount hanging over the edge at either end.

3. Tie a piece of ribbon around the ends of the paper at one end to hold it closed.

4. Fill the toilet paper roll with candy, small toys, confetti, funny sayings or "fortunes," marbles, etc.

5. Tie another piece of ribbon around the other end, closing the cracker.

6. Decorate with stickers, pictures from old gift wrap, or a child's own drawings.

7. To open, grab each end and pull!

38

Your Own House

Building a house (or a complete village or farm) out of everyday materials can provide hours of fun for all ages, from the youngest child to adults.

Here's what you'll need to get started with one house:

1 empty cardboard juice box

Paint

Craft foam

Construction paper

1 box of wooden toothpicks

Scissors

A ruler

White craft glue

Small wooden rectangles (available at craft stores)

A paintbrush

1. Wash the inside of the empty juice box carton.

2. Paint the outside of the empty box. Let the box dry completely.

3. Cut two identical roof-support triangles out of craft foam. Glue these to the top of the painted box a couple of inches apart.

4. Cut a square out of a brown grocery bag or a piece of heavy construction paper. Fold the square in half.

5. Apply strips of glue to the craft foam triangles and set the folded roof on top.

6. Glue layers of small wooden rectangles to the roof. These resemble shingles.

7. Cut doors and windows out of craft foam and glue to the front and sides of the house.

8. Use toothpicks to make windowpanes.

More Construction Tips

To make a duplex, condominium, or apartment complex, glue several boxes together. Very young children may simply draw windows and doors on the carton after an adult has covered it with brown wrapping paper.

39

Ice Candles

During the dog days of summer, it's hard to imagine that someday cooler temperatures will arrive. If you can spare some ice cubes on those hot afternoons, you can create some unusual candles called "Ice Candles." The name of these candles comes not only from the fact that ice is used to make them, but also because when left uncolored, they resemble large icicles.

To make one of these cool candles, you'll need:

Newspaper

Double boiler (or substitute a large saucepan and a large can, like a coffee can, for the double boiler)

1 lb. paraffin wax

A sharp knife (adult use only)

Crayon stubs (optional)

Empty quart-sized milk carton, washed and dried

Non-stick cooking spray

Taper candle, 7 inches long

Ice cubes, broken into large chunks

1. Cover the work area and floor with newspaper in case of spills.

2. Spray the inside of the milk carton with non-stick cooking spray. Set the carton aside.

3. Chop the wax into 1-inch chunks using a sharp knife.

4. Melt the wax over low heat in the top of a double boiler. If making a colored candle, stir in a piece of crayon stub as the wax melts. The wax should not be melted over direct heat or in a microwave.

5. When about one quarter of the wax is melted, fill the bottom 1 inch of the carton with melted wax. Insert the taper candle into the middle of the carton and hold the candle in place until the wax sets up.

6. Pack chunks of ice into the carton around the taper. Place the carton in a shallow baking dish. Set the dish aside until the rest of the wax is melted.

7. When all of the wax is melted, carefully pour it into the milk carton over the ice chunks. Fill the carton with wax so that only the tip of the taper is exposed.

8. Let candle sit for at least thirty minutes. Pour off the excess water. When the candle is completely cool, place the carton in the sink and carefully peel the carton away.

Stay cool!

Have a "candle night." Perform all of your evening activities, including preparing and eating dinner, bathing, and sharing bed-time stories by candlelight.

40

Indoor Scavenger Hunts

Scavenger hunts are always a popular activity, but they're usually held outdoors. If there's bad weather outside or you live in the middle of a city and scavenger hunts aren't feasible, don't worry. Just bring the hunt indoors!

Playing Card Scavenger Hunt

Here's a good game for a rainy day that can be fun for younger and older siblings. Grab a deck of cards and let each child choose a suit (hearts, clubs, diamonds, or spades). Hide all of the cards all over the house. (An older sibling might enjoy hiding the cards.) Then send each child off to find the cards in his or her suit. If one child is a diamond and finds a spade, she must put it back and keep looking. To make this game even more engaging, you can require the kids to find their suits in order! If one child needs a four of diamonds and she finds the five of diamonds, she must put it back, remember where it is, and come back for it after she's found the four of diamonds.

Plastic Egg Hunt

Egg hunts don't have to be just for springtime. Buy some inexpensive, brightly colored plastic eggs. For younger children, simply hide the eggs all over the house. For older kids, make it more challenging. In the first egg, write a description of where the next egg will be found. In that egg, include directions for the next location. One child can do the writing and hiding, and the others can search, or Mom and Dad can hide the eggs for all the kids.

41

Invisible
Messages

Imagine your child's surprise when she gets out of the shower to find that, as if by magic, a message has appeared out of thin air on the bathroom mirror. What a great way to wish your child a happy birthday first thing in the morning!

It's very simple to create invisible messages. You can teach even young children how to write invisible messages that will amaze and astonish their friends. These hidden messages are a fun way to send birthday wishes inside a homemade card or to invite party goers to a celebration, especially for a Halloween party. Just make sure the recipient knows how to uncover the secret message.

Beginning Ghost Writing

Preschool-aged children can create invisible notes and pictures by simply writing their message or drawing a picture on heavy white paper or white cardstock with a white crayon. The writing can be revealed by lightly coloring over the paper with a marker.

Intermediate Ghost Writing

Older kids will enjoy creating secret communiqués by writing on white paper with a cotton swab dipped in lemon juice. As the juice dries, the message will vanish into thin air. The message will re-appear when the paper is held close, but not too close, to a 100-watt light bulb, toaster, or other heat source. Parental supervision is advised for this project.

Advanced Ghost Writing

If your child takes a shower that's hot enough to steam up the mir-rors in the bathroom, you can leave a ghostly message that will appear, like magic, as the bathroom gets steamy.

Start with a clean mirror. Using cotton balls and rubbing alco-hol, or a commercial anti-fog product usually available in automo-tive departments, write a message or draw pictures on the mirror. When the steam from the shower clouds the mirror, the message will appear. To "erase" the message after it has appeared, simply wash the mirror with window cleaner.

42

A Journal and a Journal Jar

A journal is a wonderful place to record the magic of a lifetime: details of those magic moments, hopes, dreams, and sometimes just ponderings and doodles. This collection of childhood images will be a cherished memento in the years to come. Unfortunately, when faced with a blank sheet of paper, the act of recording magic memories becomes more like a task, a chore, or even homework. There are a few things you can do to make it easier for your child to record his childhood memories now and preserve them for a lifetime to come.

Before your child can journal, he needs a special place to record his memories, or whatever else comes to mind at the moment. You can use a regular notebook and pens to get started. Using scrapbook/archival quality supplies will simply help your child's journal stand the test of time. Consider purchasing a spiral-bound scrapbook with plain paper pages. These are available in a variety of sizes from 4 x 6 inches to 12 x 12 inches, and some even have black pages instead of white. Your child can decorate the cover of the scrapbook using acid-free markers and stickers. Purchase a variety of acid-free gel pens for your child to use when writing his entries; they are available in a wide range of colors, including white and other colors designed for black paper. Pick up extra stickers for use on the pages.

But the right supplies are only the tip of the iceberg. The real problem comes with *what* to write. That may be the real roadblock that keeps your child from recording his childhood memories, musings, and ponderings. If your child needs some ideas for what to write about or just a little motivation to get started, put together a journal jar for him.

To create a journal jar, you'll need a plastic jar; a recycled peanut butter jar works great. Wash the jar thoroughly, removing the label. When the jar is dry, attach a new label that says, "My Journal Jar." Or, if you're making them for several children, personalize them with "John's Journal Jar," or "Mary's Journal Jar." On 2 x 4-inch pieces of paper, write ideas or topics for your child to journal about, such as:

- If you could live anyplace in the world, where would you choose? Why?

- What is your favorite color? Why?

- What is the best day of the week? Why?

- If you could be any animal, what would you be? Why? What would a typical day be like?

- Who is the best teacher you've ever had? Why? Write that person a thank you note (in your journal).

- If you could be a character in a book, who would you pick? Why?

- What was the best gift you ever received? Why?

- What would you do if you had a million dollars?

- What do you want to do or be when you grow up?

- If you ran away with the circus, what job would you want?

- What does it mean to be a friend?

- What is the nicest thing you've ever done for someone?

- What was the scariest thing that ever happened to you?

- What is the best memory that you have from last summer?

You may want to personalize the slips based on your child's own life experiences.

Encourage your child to select a slip each time he journals or whenever he needs a little inspiration. Add additional ideas as the jar gets low. Let your child know that there are NO rules—it is his journal after all. Responses don't have to be written in essay format. He may choose to draw a picture or write a story, a poem, or a song. But do encourage him to write the question on the top of the page so that when he looks back at it years from now things will make a little more sense.

With a little help from you, your child will be on his way to collecting a lifetime of thoughts and memories. While you're making a journal jar for your child, remember that journal jars aren't just for children. If you'd like to get started on a journal of your own, or you have one, but need a little help when faced with that blank page, why not put together a journal jar for yourself? You can start with some questions you posed to your child and start collecting and recording memories of your own.

43

Make Your Own Jigsaw Puzzles

Most jigsaw puzzles are made with a big, noisy saw, but your kids will have lots of fun making their own with nothing more danger-ous than a pair of scissors. Kids (and grown-ups too!) have enjoyed piecing together these puzzles ever since the eighteenth century, when European mapmakers pasted maps onto wood, and then cut them into small pieces to make educational toys. The puzzles soared in popularity during the Great Depression as an affordable method of entertainment. Soon drugstores and libraries began renting puzzles for ten cents a day! Making your own puzzle can be delightfully fun, especially if you use a cherished family photo.

To create a wonderful toy and family memento, you'll need:
A picture or photograph (at least 8 x 10 inches)
A large flat sheet of foam board (ideal) or heavy cardboard

Dry mounting spray

A utility knife (adult use only)

1. Choose the picture for your finished puzzle. The picture can be an 8 x 10-inch favorite photo, a picture from a calendar—anything you like. However, magazine pages are too thin and tear too easily. If you have your heart set on a magazine photo, make a color copy on stiffer paper.

2. Spray the foam board or cardboard backing with dry mounting spray, available at craft or hobby stores. Follow the manufacturer's directions on the can. Lay the picture perfectly flat onto the foam board or cardboard backing with no air bubbles between the picture and the backing.

3. Cut the puzzle apart into irregularly-shaped pieces with a utility knife. Cut out the pieces slowly and carefully. Do not make pieces with tiny ends or obtrusions on them as these are likely to break off easily.

4. After cutting apart the entire picture, put the puzzle together to make sure that all of the pieces fit together properly.

Playing card puzzle

To make a super-easy puzzle, take playing cards and cut them into zigzag shapes. Mix up the pieces and see how fast you can put them together. Cut up two entire suits and race a sibling to see who can put their suit together first.

Stay cool!
For your child's next birthday party, turn the party invitations into jigsaw puzzles and mail the pieces to the guests. They'll have fun assembling the pieces to find out the party details!

44

A Little "I Love You"

Hearts and valentines aren't just for grown-ups and holidays. Kids love to give sweet mementos to the special people in their lives like grandparents, aunts and uncles, teachers, friends, and Mom and Dad. These sweetheart ideas are great ways of letting them know just how much they are loved.

A Pebble in My Pocket

Your child can create a permanent reminder of her love that a relative can keep close all the time. Using acrylic craft paint, she can embellish a small smooth stone with a tiny heart. Or add the heart to a nickel, a quarter, or even a small wooden circle. Top with a coat of clear acrylic sealer or clear nail polish. This tiny token can be carried around as a reminder of your child's love. This project is a great gift for your child to give to any special person in her life.

All Around the World

You'd go to the ends of the earth for your child, so let her know that you'll be able to say "I love you" no matter where in the world she is by learning how to say "I love you" in other languages. An Internet search will produce results for dozens and dozens of languages. Since most children are fascinated with foreign languages, this will be a fun activity for both of you. And, it's also a fun, unique way to make special "I love you" cards.

Here are a few loving phrases to get you started:
French: Je t'aime (shuh-tem)
Spanish: Te amo (tay-ah-moe)
German: Ich liebe dich (eek-leebah-deek)
Italian: Ti amo (tee-ah-moe)

Lovable Ladybugs

Create a fleet of delightful paper ladybugs and tuck them in lunch boxes, jacket pockets, and books. Simply cut small hearts out of pink or red paper, or any color your child likes. Cut small circles out of black paper. Glue the circle onto the heart, overlapping at the point. Use white gel markers to add eyes and a black marker to make a stripe and spots on the back. Write a little note on the underside of the "bug." As a great gift for a Grandma, an aunt, or other special lady, cut the shapes from craft foam, assemble, embellish, and attach a pin back.

Stay cool!

Let your child know all the things you love about him by recording them in a special book, straight from the heart. Punch two holes in the tops of a stack of heart-shaped pages. You can cut your own, pick up a heart-shaped notepad, or use scrapbook diecuts. Cut two hearts from craft foam for a front and back cover, punch holes, and assemble with binder rings.

45

Macaroni Ornaments

Is your child a *macaroni?* If this were Colonial America, he'd know you weren't calling him a piece of pasta, but a European "dandy"—a young British traveler who likes to dress up in wild clothes. Considering themselves quite elegant, these young men wore the term "macaroni" with pride during Colonial days. They liked to taunt the American Colonials by calling them Yankee Doodles. In the Dutch language, *Yankee* was a mispronunciation of the word "English," and *doodle* came from a German word meaning "simpleton." In pre-Revolutionary America, the British macaronis jeered at the colonials who thought sticking feathers in their hats was stylish, calling them Yankee Doodles. Not to be outdone, the colonials turned this into their rallying cry for independence, and the song "Yankee Doodle Dandy" was born.

Today, inexpensive macaroni comes in all shapes, sizes, and forms. It's a perfect item to craft with. This holiday season, make some Marvelous Macaroni ornaments.

You'll need:

Waxed paper
Pasta rings, thin spaghetti or linguini, and rigatoni
White craft glue
White acrylic paint
Silver or gold glitter
Ribbon or cord

1. On waxed paper, lay out a design in noodles.

2. Carefully glue pasta shapes together one at a time, and let the glue dry.

3. Paint with white acrylic paint and sprinkle on glitter before the paint dries.

4. Thread a ribbon or cord through top of the ornament and hang it wherever a little style is needed!

46

Magic Mirrors

When the first full-length animated film *Snow White and the Seven Dwarfs* was released in 1937, it prompted children of all ages to ask, "Magic Mirror on the wall, who's the fairest one of all?"

With a few supplies from a craft store, you can turn an ordinary mirror into something magical for your little prince or princess.

To get started, you'll need:

A wall mirror, with or without frame

Window cleaner

Acrylic craft paint

Glass markers or glass paint (choose a product that doesn't need to be baked or sealed)

Small glass beads, small polished stones, cabochons, small ceramic tiles

Glass glue

Flat buttons, coins, charms, faux jewels or gemstones, foam cutouts, other miscellaneous small, flat items

Paintbrushes or sponges
White craft glue or a glue gun (adult use only)

1. **Getting started:** If possible, remove the mirror from its frame. When decorating the outside edges of the mirror, remember to leave room to replace the frame. Clean the mirror with an ammonia- or alcohol-based cleaner.

2. **Paint the frame:** Use acrylic craft paint to paint the frame. Allow the paint to dry completely. If necessary, add hangers to the back of the frame.

3. **Paint the glass:** Use glass paint to decorate the glass as desired. Follow manufacturer's instructions and recommendations. Allow the paint to dry completely.

4. **Embellish the glass:** Use glass glue to adhere items to the mirror as desired. If you use small beads, string them before gluing to the mirror, and then remove the string after the glue has dried.

5. **Embellish the frame:** As desired, glue a variety of small, flat items to the frame. For best results, use hot glue or thick, white craft glue. If the craft glue is thin, allow the bottle to sit open for at least an hour before using it. Allow the glue to dry completely.

6. Putting it all together: Insert the mirror back into the frame and secure the mirror in place. Hang or mount the mirror at eye level.

Once the mirror is in place, spend some time with your child filling a large box with old purses, scarves, jewelry, ties, gowns, shoes (athletic shoes, sandals, and high heels), shirts, hats (child-sized versions of a hard hat, a sailor's hat, a nurse's cap, a firefighter's helmet, and a police officer's hat), and athletic equipment (football helmets, hockey masks, and jerseys). You can also create items to add to the box: use thin cardboard or craft foam to make masks (animals, animated characters, cartoon characters, aliens, or favorite literary characters), crowns, and other accessories. Once the box is full, invite several of your child's friends over for an afternoon of fun. As the children complete a new look, invite them to check themselves out in the magic mirror. Document the children's transformations with photos or video. If possible, use a digital or instant camera for several of the shots, which make not only great party favors, but permanent reminders of the fun.

Stay cool!

Use your favorite technique or techniques to decorate a picture frame as a special gift for a grandparent or long-distance friend. Insert a favorite picture of you and the recipient before giving it. These frames are also a great way to frame some of your child's favorite memories from the dress-up party.

47

Mail

The United States Postal Service delivers more than 200 billion pieces of mail a year, and each letter carrier carries an average of 2,300 pieces of mail a day. Most of the packages are humdrum, but do you know that you can send a party invitation in a "road map" envelope, a birthday present in a paint can, or a secret message in a bottle? It's perfectly legal. Mail doesn't *have* to be sent in a tidy white envelope. With a few supplies and just a couple of minutes, you can make someone's mailbox (and their mail carrier) smile!

The Envelope, Please

From a piece of wrapping paper, wallpaper, decorative craft paper, or a map, cut a 9-inch square. Lightly pencil in a diagonal line from the left top corner to the bottom right corner on the back of the paper. Draw another diagonal line from the right top corner to the bottom left corner. Cut a cardboard rectangle 4-1/2 inches tall and 5-3/4 inches wide. Draw a line straight down from the center of the top of the cardboard to the bottom. Draw a second straight line from the center of the left side to the center of the right side. Lay the paper down with the diagonal lines facing up. Place the cardboard on the top of the paper, and match up the lines on the cardboard and the paper. Fold the sides of the paper in, and then fold the bottom up. Using tape or glue stick, secure the bottom flap of the paper to the sides. Fold the top flap down along the cardboard. Remove the cardboard and insert your card or letter. Seal the envelope with tape or glue stick.

Canned Goods

Decorate the outside of an unused quart-sized paint can with stickers. Unused paint cans are often available at home improvement or paint stores. Attach a mailing label to the can. Put your parcels into the paint can and use packing peanuts or tissue paper to protect the items. Place the lid on the can and tap it down with a hammer. Be careful not to make the can too heavy or it will be very expensive to send.

Message in a Bottle

Remove the label from a 1- or 2-liter plastic soda or water bottle. Rinse out the bottle and allow it to dry completely. Simply roll up a note and slip it into the mouth of the bottle. This is a fun way to send party invitations or secret, coded messages.

You can send more than just messages in a bottle, too. Insert small items into the bottle through the mouth, alternating the items with packing peanuts. Fill any extra space with packing peanuts. For larger items, make a slit in the bottle long enough to slip the items through. Stuff the item in and pack securely around it. Place a piece of clear packing tape over the slit.

Attach a mailing label to the bottle. If you've made a slit, place the label over the slit and secure it again with more packing tape.

Stay cool!

Use the mail to brighten the day of some very sick kids by sending them cards, letters, or small gifts. For more information, check out the Make a Child Smile program at http://www.makeachildsmile.org.

48

Maple Ice Candy

It takes about forty gallons of sap to make one gallon of maple syrup. The sap is cooked down and most of the water in the sap is evaporated until the sugary liquid is one-third water and two-thirds sugar. This sweet treat is the perfect topper for a stack of pancakes. It's also great on a bowl of vanilla ice cream.

The syrup can be cooked down further and made into candy or poured over snow or shaved ice to make "sugar-on-snow." A springtime favorite for more than two hundred years, this treat is traditionally served with dill pickles, saltine crackers, or plain doughnuts.

To make a sweet treat that's slightly crunchier but similar to sugar-on-snow, you'll need:

A bottle of 100% pure maple syrup

Lots of ice

A candy thermometer

Waxed paper

9 x 13-inch pan

2- or 3-quart saucepan

1. Use a blender or electric ice crusher to crush enough ice to pack a 9 x 13-inch pan about half full. (If you have access to clean snow, you can pack that into the pan instead of crushed ice.) Put the pan in the freezer.

2. Pour 1 cup of syrup into a 2-quart or 3-quart saucepan. It foams up a lot during the cooking process. Attach the candy thermometer to the inside of the saucepan.

3. Cook over medium heat, stirring occasionally, until it reaches 244°F/118°C (firm ball consistency) on the candy thermometer.

4. Remove the saucepan from the heat. Remove the pan of ice from the freezer. Carefully pour the syrup onto the ice using a large spoon or a ladle. (Be careful! The syrup will be very hot.)

5. When the candy has cooled off, use a fork to remove it from the ice and set it on a sheet of waxed paper.

6. Break the candy into bite-sized pieces and enjoy.

7. Store any extra candy on sheets of waxed paper in an air-tight container in the refrigerator.

This candy is very sticky and quite chewy. For a hard, rock-type candy, heat the syrup until it reaches 300°F/149°C (hard crack consistency) on the candy thermometer. For a softer taffy candy, cook it to soft ball consistency (234°F/112°C). Experiment heating the syrup to different levels until you find the version your family likes best.

Stay cool!

Visit a "sugarhouse" or "sugar bush" (the building where the sap is cooked down) and watch maple syrup being made. If that's not an option, stop by the library to check out *Sugaring* by Jessie Haas (author) and Joseph Smith (illustrator).

49

Marbled Ornaments

Most children are content to craft with whatever supplies are on hand or whatever they can scrounge up. But with the right materials, even children in the early elementary grades can create beautiful works of art like the "marbled ornaments" described below. They can be used to adorn the branches of a Christmas tree or hung by long ribbons in a window for a stunning effect.

To make these marbled masterpieces, you'll need:
A small paper cup

Vinegar

A clear glass ornament

Acrylic craft paint, 3 or more colors

1/4-inch satin ribbon

1. Remove the cap and hanger from the glass ornament. Rinse the inside of the ornament with a mixture of equal parts vinegar and water. Let the ornaments dry completely.

2. Squeeze a small amount of paint into the ornament. Turn, rotate, or shake the ornament to distribute the paint. (Have your kids be careful of sharp edges on the top of the glass ornament!)

3. Add another color. Shake and turn the ornament.

4. Repeat for the rest of the colors you want to use. Add additional paint as needed.

5. Continue moving the ornament to distribute the paint until the inside is completely covered.

6. Turn the ornament upside down (stem down) in a paper cup to drain until all the excess paint has dripped out. This may take a few days, depending on how much excess paint is in the ornament.

7. Replace the cap and hanger and add a ribbon for hanging.

50

Homemade Marshmallows

Whether mashed into s'mores, floated in a big mug of hot cocoa, or roasted over a campfire, marshmallows have been a childhood favorite since about 1850. You can make this treat in your own kitchen. And when you do, you can add coloring and flavoring that will turn ordinary marshmallows into something very cool.

To make this confection at home, you'll need:

Non-stick cooking spray

1/3 cup powdered sugar

1/4 cup cornstarch

1 packet unflavored gelatin

1-1/2 cups water, divided into two 3/4 cup portions

2-1/2 cups white sugar

Vanilla or flavored oil

Food coloring (optional)

8 x 8-inch pan
A saucepan
A large mixing bowl
An electric mixer
A candy thermometer

1. Sift together the cornstarch and powdered sugar.

2. Spray an 8 x 8-inch pan with nonstick spray. Put 1 or 2 tablespoons of the cornstarch and powdered sugar mixture into the bottom of the pan. Tilt the pan, covering the bottom and sides completely. Leave any excess powder in the pan. Set the pan aside.

3. Measure 3/4 cup water into a large bowl. Sprinkle the gelatin over the water. Set the bowl aside.

4. In a saucepan, mix together the sugar and remaining 3/4 cup water. Cook over medium heat, stirring occasionally, until the mixture reaches 230°F/110°C (thread consistency) on the candy thermometer.

5. Pour the syrup into the bowl, over the gelatin. Let the syrup cool slightly.

6. Add 1/4 teaspoon of vanilla or other flavor and a few drops of food coloring if desired.

7. Using an electric mixer, beat the mixture until stiff peaks form.

8. Pour the mixture into the powdered pan. Use a spatula to smooth the top. Let this sit for about two hours until the mixture is set.

9. Cut the marshmallow concoction into squares with a wet knife. Cut around the outer edge of the pan to loosen the contents.

10. Sprinkle the remaining cornstarch and powdered sugar mixture onto a cutting board.

11. Turn the marshmallows onto the cutting board. Roll the marshmallows so that all surfaces get covered with the mixture.

12. Let the marshmallows air-dry overnight on a wire rack covered with paper towels. Store in an airtight container.

51

Memory Cards

If your kids have trouble remembering what happened to their lunch money or their mittens, you may want to help them brush up on their memory skills. Playing with Memory Cards is a great activity for kids of any age; they'll have fun making the cards first and then playing the game afterwards!

To make a set of memory cards, you'll need:

Cardboard (gift boxes or cereal boxes)

Construction paper

Scissors

White craft glue

Crayons or markers

A ruler

Laminating pages (optional)

1. Cut the gift box so that it is just a plain, flat surface the same size as the piece of construction paper.

2. Glue the paper onto the cardboard.

3. Use the ruler to make an *even* number of equal-sized squares.

4. Draw one picture in one of the squares, and draw a duplicate picture in the square next to it. Continue drawing duplicate pictures until all of the squares are filled. For example, draw two circles in two boxes, another two with a cat face, and another two with a moon—whatever your child might like to see or draw.

5. Cut out each individual square.

6. Laminate each card, if you wish. Simply place each card between two laminating pages and press down. Laminated cards are much longer lasting!

TO PLAY: Turn the cards face down and mix them up. Line them up in even rows. Take turns turning over two cards to try to make a match. When a child makes a match, she takes both cards. Cards that don't match are turned face down again, and play moves to the next child. The winner is the child with the most cards in her pile after all of the cards have been matched.

Stay cool!

Instead of drawing pictures on the memory cards, photocopy old family pictures or scan them into a computer and print them out, making sure all the photos are the same size. Laminate the photo-copies if you wish and play the memory game with your child's family or friends!

52

A Memory Quilt

Imagine presenting your new daughter-in-law with a quilt on the day she marries your son, or packing a handmade quilt in with your daughter's belongings when she heads off to college. But these are not just any quilts, they're made by you and your child featuring his or her artwork!

Start by having your child create a quilt panel once a year, such as on New Year's Day or a birthday. By the time your child is eighteen, you'll have enough panels to create a magical memory quilt featuring pictures your child has drawn over the years. Or, collect a picture every month and stitch the perfect gift for any grandparent. If you don't quilt, you can turn the panels into a pillow or frame them.

To make these fabric masterpieces, you'll need:
Muslin fabric

Freezer paper (not waxed paper)

Crayons

Black permanent fabric pen (Check with a fabric or quilting shop for a product designed for writing on muslin. Experiment on a scrap of fabric before writing or marking on the panel.)

A clothes iron

1. Wash and dry fabric without fabric softener, then iron.

2. Cut a quilt panel from the muslin. Keep in mind that you can always trim the panels a bit if they are too big.

3. Place the shiny, plastic side of the freezer paper against the fabric. Use a warm iron to adhere the piece of freezer paper to the muslin. This will add stability to the fabric, which will make it easier for your child to work on.

4. Let your child color the panel with crayons directly on the fabric. Use the fabric pen to add details. Be sure to have your child sign and date the panel.

5. Lay a double thickness of paper toweling on top of the panel and heat-set the panel using a hot, dry iron.

6. When the fabric is cool, peel the freezer paper from the back.

Older kids, who might think they are too "cool" to color an original picture, can use a picture from a coloring book as a guide. There are some great books on the market with very detailed, interesting designs. Tape the picture to the back of the freezer paper and use the fabric pen to trace the design. You can hold the fabric and pattern against a window and let the sun illuminate the pattern for easier tracing. Once the outline is in place, your child can fill in the details with crayon.

53

A Mini-Garden

To spend some quiet time with your children, consider turning left-over TV-dinner trays or tins from frozen pies into a miniature garden or ocean scene. You can also buy inexpensive disposable aluminum pans that work just as well. Kids of all ages find something to enjoy in this creative activity.

Send your kids out to the park, backyard, or a garden to hunt for twigs to make trees, moss for a lawn, and small stones. You'll need to have a little blue tack on hand. When your youngsters get back from their scavenger expedition, here's what they'll do:

1. Cement twigs or stones in place with a little blue tack.

2. Place moss for a lawn and sprinkle stones for rockery or a little waterfall.

3. Add toy people or animals.

4. If the container is watertight, add a "pond" by fashioning

aluminum foil into a saucer shape; cover edges with rocks and/or moss. Add water.

Beach Variation

If your kids love the ocean, have them create a beach scene instead. They can use sand from the beach if they have any. Play sand also works well. Don't use builder's sand, which will stain yellow. Use an old fork to rake the sand into position. Add small shells and stones and a blue paper sea.

54

A Money Can

If money seems to slip through your kids' fingers, how about letting them create their own cool bank to corral that spare change?

To make this bank, you'll need:
An empty coffee can with a plastic lid
Paper
Markers, paint, or crayons
Decoupage glue (such as ModPodge)
A utility knife (adult use only)

1. Measure the circumference of the coffee can and cut the paper to fit the outside of the can.

2. Create a design on the paper.

3. Paint the back of the paper with decoupage glue and wrap the paper around the container. Allow the glue to dry.

4. Coat the outside of the can with another layer of the glue.

5. Cut a slit in the plastic lid for money to slip through.

Stay cool!

Most banks won't open a checking account for kids under age 16. One that will is the Young Americans Center for Financial Education in Denver, the first (and only) bank just for young people. Your child can get checking and savings accounts, credit cards, and small business loans—in person or through the mail—with extensive counseling and education.
Check out: www.theyoungamericans.org or call
at (303) 321-2265.

55

Morning Muffins

We all know that breakfast is the most important meal of the day, but some mornings it may seem that getting your child to eat a good breakfast is easier said than done. In between finding homework assignments, tennis shoes, and jackets before it's time to leave, forget about baking anything from scratch for breakfast!

The magic in these cereal-based muffins lies in the fact that you and your child can prepare these the night before and store them in the refrigerator. In the morning, you can pop them in the oven before you jump into the shower and the whole family can enjoy fresh-from-the-oven muffins.

To make these tasty time-savers, you'll need:

Non-stick cooking spray

2-1/2 cups raisin bran cereal

1-1/4 cups all-purpose flour

3/4 cup sugar

1 tsp. baking soda

1/4 cup unsweetened applesauce

1/4 cup egg substitute

1 cup milk; rice or soy milk can be substituted

A muffin pan

A toothpick

The night before:

1. In a large bowl, mix together the cereal, flour, sugar, and baking soda.

2. Add in the applesauce, egg substitute, and milk. Stir well until the dry ingredients are moist.

3. Cover and refrigerate overnight.

When you're ready to bake:

1. Preheat the oven to 400°F. Spray the wells of a muffin pan with non-stick cooking spray. Set the pan aside.

2. Stir the batter.

3. Fill the wells of the muffin pan two-thirds full. Any leftover batter can be stored in the refrigerator for up to a week.

4. Bake for 18 to 20 minutes or until a toothpick inserted in the center of a muffin comes out clean.

Stay cool!

Surprise your child with breakfast in bed to celebrate a birthday, a snow day, or for no reason at all! Prepare a tray with a muffin, a glass of juice, and some of your child's other breakfast favorites. Round out the tray with the morning's funny pages, a comic book, a word search book, or the latest installment in your child's favorite series.

56

No-Bake Cookies

The smell of no-bake cookies, a combination of chocolate, peanut butter, and oatmeal, takes most parents right back to the hallowed halls of middle school, where no-bake cookies were a bake sale favorite. But these perennial favorites aren't just for bake sales, even though they are a great solution if you are called upon for a contribution at the last moment. They are a great treat anytime, especially those days when it's too hot to heat up the kitchen by baking a batch of cookies in the oven.

To make these quick-and-easy favorites, you'll need:

1 stick margarine

2 cups sugar

1/2 cup milk

1/2 cup cocoa powder

1 tsp. vanilla

1/2 cup peanut butter

3-1/2 cups quick oats

A cookie sheet

A large saucepan

1. Cover a large cookie sheet with waxed paper. Set the cookie sheet aside.

2. Combine the margarine, sugar, milk, and cocoa powder in a large saucepan.

3. Over medium heat, bring the mixture to a full, rolling boil. Boil for one minute.

4. Remove the pan from the heat and stir in the vanilla, peanut butter, and quick oats.

5. Place spoonfuls of the mixture onto the cookie sheet. Let the cookies cool at room temperature. Store them in an airtight container.

57

Painted Leaf Prints

Each autumn, most trees lose their leaves as a part of their preparation for winter. In fact, that's why this time of year is also known as "fall." In many parts of the country, the leaves turn fiery shades of red, yellow, orange, burgundy, rust, and brown, creating a fabulous once-a-year display. You can capture a little bit of the splendor of the season by making imprints of the leaves on T-shirts, sweatshirts, pillowcases, tote bags, and note cards—the possibilities are endless.

To recreate the colors of autumn, you'll need:

A white or light colored T-shirt, sweatshirt, pillowcase, apron, or canvas tote bag

A large piece of thick cardboard

Brushable fabric paint or acrylic craft paint and textile/fabric medium

Foam brushes, 1 for each color of paint
Paper plates
Newspaper
White office paper
Small ink roller (or tin can)

1. Wash and dry non-canvas items *without* fabric softener.

2. Cut a piece of cardboard to fit inside the shirt or pillowcase. If possible, cut the cardboard so that it's a tight fit.

3. On a dry day, collect a variety of leaves. For best results, select freshly-fallen leaves that are not brittle. If the leaves are damp, dry them on paper toweling.

4. Mix the acrylic paint with the textile/fabric medium on a paper plate. Acrylic paint on fabric may crack or peel if it is not combined with textile medium.

5. Place a leaf on a piece of newspaper and apply some paint to the leaf with a foam brush.

6. Lay the leaf paint-side down on your T-shirt or other item. Place a piece of white paper over the top of the leaf and roll over the leaf with a small ink roller or tin can. Consider practicing this process before you apply any paint to your T-shirt or other item.

7. Make as many leaf prints on the item as desired.

8. Allow the project to dry, and heat-set according to the paint manufacturer's instructions.

Stay cool!

Press extra leaves for other projects. Clip off the stems at the base of the leaves. Place leaves between the pages of a large phone book or stack of large books. Leave them there for a week or two, or until the leaves turn papery. Remove the leaves and adhere them to note cards or scrapbook pages or mount them on pieces of card stock and hang them in a frame.

58

Homemade Paper

Kids are very curious about how things are made. What could be more magical than creating something they use every day: paper! This project is a good way to recycle old tests and discarded drawings into new works of art. To make this recycled product, you can use any type of used paper or a combination of different types. Experiment with office paper, notebook paper, construction paper, paper towels, tissue paper, or newspaper. Be aware that a high concentration of printed newspaper will produce paper with a grey tint.

To make a batch of paper perfect for cards, journal pages, or even frame-worthy art, you'll need:

Used paper

A large bowl

A blender

A large rectangular plastic wash tub

1-1/2 gallons of warm water

Liquid starch (at least 2 tbsp.)

Food coloring, glitter, pieces of string, yarn, or embroidery floss, flower petals, leaves, blades of grass (optional)

A piece of window screen or plastic craft canvas

2 pieces of felt, larger than the window screen or plastic canvas

A stack of newspaper

A rolling pin

A colander

Clothes iron (optional)

1. Tear the used paper into small pieces and soak them in a large bowl of warm water until soft.

2. Put about 2 cups warm water in the blender. Add paper until the blender is about two-thirds full. Blend the paper and water to a smooth consistency.

3. Mix together about a gallon of warm water and 2 tablespoons liquid starch in the plastic wash basin. Stir in the paper from the blender. This mixture is called a "slurry."

4. Stir in some food coloring, glitter, pieces of string, and/or bits of flower petals, leaves, or blades of grass.

5. Insert the screen or plastic canvas into the wash tub under the slurry. Lift up some of the slurry, trying to get a thin, even coat on the screen or canvas. It might help to have an extra set of hands for this step.

6. Hold the screen or canvas over the wash tub and let some of the water drain.

7. Set the screen or canvas on a stack of newspapers with a piece of felt on top. Place the other piece of felt and more newspaper on top.

8. Roll over this stack with a rolling pin to remove as much water as possible.

9. Remove the newspaper and felt and slowly and carefully remove the wet piece of newly created paper.

10. Set the paper in a warm location to dry completely. An adult can use a hot iron to speed this process if desired.

11. Use a colander to drain any leftover slurry and discard this gunk in the trash. Do not dump the mixture down the drain!

Stay cool!

You can use this method as a fun way of planting flowers for little ones, using special paper that will grow flowers! Follow the instructions listed above for making paper, omitting the starch. After removing the slurry, sprinkle flower seeds over the top before pressing the canvas or screen between the felt and newspaper. Do not dry this paper with an iron.

Use this paper to send a special, fun, springtime message to a friend across town or across the country. Be sure to let your friend know to plant the note for an extra surprise. For an added touch, cut the paper in the shape of a flower before writing your note.

59

"Paper" Dolls

Paper dolls and other toys made from paper have been popular toys since they were first mass-produced in the 1800s. During the first half of the twentieth century, paper dolls appeared in a number of women's and children's magazines. Parents and grandparents might remember Betsy McCall, who first appeared in *McCall's* magazine in 1951.

With all of the entertainment options available today, it's possible your child has never played with paper dolls. You can use your home computer to make durable paper dolls whose clothing is not held on by tabs, but by magnetism. In fact, with just a little extra effort, you can make paper dolls that look just like your child and her friends.

To make a set of these magical playmates, you'll need:

Printable magnetic sheets for inkjet printers

Paper doll template (optional)

Permanent markers

Small scraps of fabric, ribbon, yarn, small buttons, and other miscellaneous embellishments

White craft glue

A cookie sheet (makes a great play board for the magnetic paper dolls)

"Generic" Friends

There are hundreds of paper dolls ready to print and cut on the Internet. To get started, use a search engine (such as www.google.com) to search for "paper dolls." Once you find a paper doll that your child likes, you can usually print directly from the website onto the magnetic sheets. If you don't have Internet access or a printer, you can trace a paper doll template from a craft store directly onto the magnetic sheets.

After your child cuts out the doll and clothing from the magnetic sheets, she can use permanent markers to color or add details. Embellish the clothing by gluing on small buttons, ribbon, scraps of fabric, and more.

A Friend Like Me

To turn your child into a doll, select a paper doll template from the Internet and print it on white paper or get a template from a craft store. Cut out a picture of your child's face and hair, approximately the same size as the head of the paper doll. Attach the picture to the doll. Scan the image into your computer and print it on a magnetic sheet. Go to a commercial copy shop if you don't have the necessary computer equipment. Repeat with pictures of your child's friends to make additional buddies for your child's magnet image. If your child has a favorite actor or singer, you can scan his or her face onto a paper doll, too.

60

Party Platters

A scrumptious-looking cake, frosted in the birthday child's favorite color and topped with candy and other treats, is the centerpiece of many birthday celebrations. Add to the celebration by serving the cake on a party platter hand-painted by the birthday child. If time permits, she also could paint a plate for each of the partygoers to take home after the cake has been eaten.

To make these creative cake servers, you'll need:

Clear glass plate or platter
Pattern and masking tape
Grease pencil or china marker
Glass paint and brushes

There are several types of glass paints on the market specifically for painting on glass dinnerware. Some of these seal the paint with a topcoat while others require baking in the oven. If possible, experiment with several products. Select the one that gives you the best results, or the one that you find the easiest to work with. For best results, follow all manufacturer's instructions and recommendations for the product you select.

Caution: While these products are nontoxic, they should not touch food, drink, or your mouth. Paint on the *underside* of the plate. To create useable bowls, glasses, or mugs, paint on the outside of the items, leaving about 1 inch unpainted around the top rim.

1. Wash your plate in hot, soapy water. Rinse completely. Allow the plate to dry thoroughly. Prepare the surface as indicated on product instructions.

2. Make a reverse image copy of your pattern. Tape the reverse image of the pattern to the top of the plate and turn the plate over, tracing the image onto the back of the plate with the china marker.

3. Alternatively, sketch a design onto the back of the plate with the pencil or marker.

4. Paint the back of the plate as desired.

5. Follow the manufacturer's directions for drying times, plus sealing or baking instructions.

6. Leave your project in the oven after baking, if applicable, until the plate is completely cool. As a general rule, glass

items will break when placed into a hot oven. Most manu-facturers recommend placing your item into a cold oven and then allowing it to come up to temperature along with the oven.

Stay cool!

Celebrate the weekend before or after your child's birthday each year by creating a new plate. Paint additional pieces, including bowls, mugs or glasses, and other serving pieces throughout the year. By the time your child is ready to set up his first household, he will have a special set of dinnerware created through the years with love.

61

Peanut Butter Balls

Peanut butter is the second most recognizable smell, according to Yale University researchers (coffee is number one). According to the Peanut Advisory Board, Americans consume about 700 million pounds of peanut butter a year—about three pounds for every man, woman, and child!

November is Peanut Butter Lover's month. You can celebrate with your child and a batch of peanut butter balls. This is a great recipe for even the youngest helpers.

To make these bite-sized peanut butter delights, you'll need:

1 stick butter or margarine

1 (18 oz.) jar creamy peanut butter

1 pound powdered sugar (4 cups)

2 cups chocolate chips (12 oz. package)

1/2 block edible paraffin wax (baker's wax)
Waxed paper
A saucepan
A cookie sheet

1. Cover a large cookie sheet with waxed paper. Set the cookie sheet aside.

2. In a large saucepan, melt the butter over medium heat. Add the peanut butter. Stir constantly until the peanut butter is melted and the mixture is smooth. Remove the pan from the heat.

3. Slowly add the powdered sugar. Stir well, breaking up any lumps of powdered sugar, until the dough is no longer sticky and will hold its shape when formed into balls.

4. When the dough is cool enough to work with, roll it into 1-inch balls and place on the prepared cookie sheet. Insert a toothpick into the center of each ball. Put the cookie sheet in the refrigerator until the balls have cooled.

5. Melt the paraffin wax and chocolate chips together over low heat. Dip the balls into the chocolate mixture. Cool the treats on waxed paper.

6. Store them in an airtight container in the refrigerator.

Stay cool!

Make some lunchtime magic with sandwiches made with home-made peanut butter. Shell and remove the red skins from dry roasted peanuts. You'll need at least 1/2 cup of shelled peanuts. Grind the nuts in a blender, mini-chopper, or food processor. Add about 1 teaspoon of peanut or vegetable oil. Process until smooth, adding additional oil as necessary. Salt to taste. Store in the refrigerator in an airtight container for up to two weeks.

62

Piñatas

Filled with candy, toys, and other surprises, piñatas are a favorite among children. In Mexico, children get to break open a piñata on each of the nine days before Christmas. These days are called *Las Posadas* and are a time of celebration and feasting. Piñatas are also found at many Cinco de Mayo parties. Your child can make a festively colored piñata for your next party. But you don't need to wait for a reason to throw a party. Make a piñata and invite your child's friends over for a backyard barbeque.

To make this smashingly fun party favor, you'll need:

A balloon, 12 to 16 inches in diameter

Newsprint (unprinted newsprint is much cleaner—see if your local newspaper will give you an unprinted roll end)

White craft or school glue

An empty jar with a lid

A razor blade knife (adult use only)

An empty paper towel or toilet tissue roll (any cardboard tube)

Masking tape
Acrylic craft paint and brushes or sponges
String
A shallow bowl

1. Cut newsprint into strips 1 to 2 inches wide and 3 to 4 inches long.

2. Inflate the balloon. Set the balloon aside.

3. Combine 2 parts craft or school glue and 1 part warm tap water in the jar. Replace the lid and shake vigorously until the water and glue are mixed well. Pour the paste into a shallow bowl.

4. Dip the paper strips into the paste. Squeeze away any excess paste by pulling the strip between two fingers. Cover the balloon with one or two layers of paper strips, leaving a small area around the stem uncovered. Set the balloon aside to dry overnight. Pour the paste back into the jar and replace the lid tightly. Shake the paste mixture again before using.

5. Using masking tape, securely tape a 2-inch piece of the cardboard tube to the top of the balloon around the stem area. Cover the balloon and the tube with one or two additional layers of pasted strips. Use several extra layers of

strips to help attach the tube to the piñata. Set it aside to dry completely.

6. Use a razor blade knife (adults only!) to cut a three-sided opening, like a small door, in the back of the piñata. The balloon will have popped by the time you've finished this step.

7. Remove the balloon pieces, fill the piñata with candy and toys, and tape the small door shut.

8. Paint and decorate the piñata. You can turn it into a smiley face, a soccer ball, a pumpkin, a basketball, a baseball, a mouse, a spider, a globe, an octopus, or just about anything you can imagine.

9. To hang the piñata, make two holes opposite one another about halfway down each side of the cardboard stem. Thread a piece of string through the holes, tie the ends together, and hang the piñata from a hook or a tree.

63

Plane Entertainment

The thought of spending five or six hours on a plane might not seem like much of a good time, but it's possible to turn those air-time hours into some really magical moments if you spend a little time preparing. Before you go, talk with your child about planes and flight. Introduce chats about the Wright brothers, Charles Lindbergh, Amelia Earhart, or Beryl Markham.

Space is limited on a plane and you can't spread out to entertain, so it's best if you can store entertainment items in a child's backpack. (This has the added benefit of providing a backpack once you get to your destination for hands-free exploring.)

Take some books about famous fliers along on the trip. Consider *A Picture Book of Amelia Earhart* by David A. Adler, *Lost Star: The Story of Amelia Earhart* by Patricia Lauber; *The Wright Brothers for Kids— How They Invented the Airplane: 21 Activities Exploring the Science and History of Flight* by Mary Kay Carson; and *Night Flight: Charles*

Lindbergh's Incredible Adventure by Sydelle A. Kramer. Older children might enjoy the lyrical *West with the Night* by Beryl Markham.

Air travel isn't as luxurious as it used to be and many flights won't offer much more fuel for your body than a sack of pretzels and a soda. Here are some great items to be sure to pack into each child's backpack:

- Individual applesauce and fruit cups (don't forget plastic spoons)

- Dry crackers (small snack-pack size)

- Small water bottles (label the bottles with a permanent marker to keep these separate for each child)

- Individual-serving cereal boxes

- Flavored rice cakes

- Juice boxes

- Small box of animal crackers

Travel Game Printouts

If you're Internet savvy, you can find lots of websites featuring printable travel games, such as connect-the-dot games, word searches, coloring pictures, word scrambles, and much, much more. Visit the parents travel section at www.activitiesforkids.com.

64

Powdered Drink Mix

Like most inventors, Edwin E. Perkins probably hoped for the best when he introduced his "Kool-Ade" (later changed to Kool-Aid) in 1927. Originally available in seven flavors, the one-ounce packages that sold for ten cents each were an instant hit. By 1950, the Chicago factory that produced the drink mix was churning out nearly a million packets a day.

Perkins most likely never suspected how many uses those little packets could have—everything from dying yarn to flavoring cake frosting. Pick up a few of your child's favorite flavors and make some magic together with these really "kool" projects.

Flavored Lip Gloss

With just a couple ingredients from the pantry and a few minutes, your child can mix up some flavored lip gloss right in your own kitchen. In a small, microwave-safe bowl, melt 1 tablespoon solid vegetable shortening, microwaving in ten second intervals until complete. Stir in 1 tablespoon powdered drink mix with sugar added. Mix for a minute or two until smooth. Carefully spoon into a lip gloss pot and refrigerate until solid.

Candied Popcorn

Use your favorite drink mix flavor to make candied popcorn. This recipe works best if you make your own popcorn. In a 3-quart covered pan, put 3 tablespoons liquid vegetable oil and a couple of kernels of unpopped popcorn. With the lid in place, heat the oil over medium high heat until the kernels pop. Carefully add 1/3 to 1/2 cup unpopped kernels. Replace the lid and gently shake the pan until the popping stops. Carefully remove the lid from the pan and pour the popcorn into a large bowl. Sprinkle 1/4 to 1/2 cup powdered drink mix (with sugar added) over the top of the popcorn. Toss well. Add additional drink mix as desired. Be sure to have some baby wipes handy to clean up those sticky fingers, big and small!

Watercolor Art

Powdered drink mix isn't just for edible projects. You can make your own watercolors to create beautiful works of art! Put 1 cup warm water in a clean plastic or glass jar with a lid, such as a peanut butter jar. Add 1 package unsweetened drink mix powder. Replace the lid and shake until the powder is completely dissolved. Adjust the amount of powder to create lighter and darker shades.

Paint on watercolor paper. For an abstract look, pour the colored water in spray bottles and squirt it onto the paper. Experiment with different colors and various nozzle settings.

Stay cool!

Check out pages 14-16 in *Kids Knitting* by Melanie Falick for simple directions on how to dye wool yarn using your favorite colors of powdered drink mix. When your yarn is done, learn how to knit or crochet (if you don't already know how), and create a really "kool" one-of-a-kind scarf.

65

Homemade Pretzels

Pretzels were created long ago in the seventh century when a young monk in southern France prepared unleavened bread for Lent. It was the custom back then to pray with the arms folded across the chest, each hand on the opposite shoulder. The monk decided to twist leftover bread dough into this shape to use as a treat for the children. He named his creation *Pretiola* (Latin for "little reward"), and a snack food was born. The center of pretzel history in America is Lititz, Pennsylvania, where the first commercial pretzel bakery was founded in 1861. Up to that date, pretzels were always baked until they were soft, like bread. But in the 19th century, a Lititz baker's apprentice dozed off while baking soft pretzels, and mistakenly baked them twice as long as necessary. When the master baker found out, he was outraged—until he tasted one. To his delight, he discovered they were crisp and tasty, and the new hard pretzels also retained their freshness much longer.

To make your own version of *Pretiola*, you'll need:

1 cup warm water

4 cups room-temperature water

1 package dry active yeast

2-3/4 cups flour, divided into 1-1/2 cup and 1-1/4 cup portions

2 tbsp. vegetable oil

1/2 tsp. table salt

2 tbsp. coarse salt

4 cups water

2 tbsp. baking soda

1. Dissolve the yeast in 1 cup warm water and let stand for ten minutes.

2. Add the vegetable oil, table salt, and 1-1/2 cups flour, and stir until thoroughly combined.

3. Add the remaining 1-1/4 cups flour and knead the dough for 5 minutes.

4. Cover the dough with a cloth and let it rest for one hour.

5. Divide the dough into twelve equal pieces and form them into small balls. Let them rest for 15 minutes.

6. Roll the dough balls into 18-inch lengths and form into pretzel shapes, or cut each length in half to make sticks.

7. Let the pretzels rise for 30 minutes.

8. Preheat the oven to 475°F.

9. In a large pot, mix the baking soda and 4 cups water. Bring the mixture to a boil. Add the pretzels to the boiling water for one minute.

10. Remove the pretzels and place them on a greased cookie sheet.

11. Sprinkle with the coarse salt and bake for 12 minutes.

66

Pumpkin Carving

Whether you want to carve a pumpkin to decorate the porch on Halloween night or hold a pumpkin-carving party with your friends and family, pumpkin carving is a wonderful way for you and the kids to have fun together.

Folks have been carving vegetables for Halloween ever since the time of the ancient Celts, when the holiday was known as Samhain. October 31 was considered to be the end of the Celtic year and a night to honor loved ones who had died. On this magical night, glowing jack-o-lanterns were carved from turnips and set out to welcome old relatives and protect against evil spirits. Burning lumps of coal were used inside as a source of light, which were later replaced by candles. When Irish settlers arrived in America they found the native pumpkin was bigger and easier to carve, and a tradition was born. Here's how to make some pumpkin fun of your own!

Choose Your Pumpkin

Not just any gourd will do. Very large pumpkins can be carved with elaborate designs and used as a centerpiece on your porch or dinner table. Medium-sized pumpkins work best if you're using stencils. You can get away with a small pumpkin for carving traditional faces, and then scatter them around for party decorations or along the sidewalk as a lighted pathway. Select ripe pumpkins that are uniformly orange, without any bruises, cuts, or nicks. Never carry a pumpkin by its stem, and try not to bruise the skin while you carry it home; bruising will shorten its lifespan.

Ready...Set...Carve!

1. With a long, thin bladed knife, cut out the top of the pumpkin around the stem of the pumpkin, either as a round circle or a five-sided opening. As you cut out the hole, angle the knife so that the lid is cone-shaped. This helps keep the lid from falling into the hole.

2. Using a big spoon, scrape the inside walls clean.

3. Outline the design of the face by using a crayon or marker onto the surface of the pumpkin. Young children may be happy simply decorating their pumpkin with crayons or markers, and gluing on sequins, feathers, or scraps of cloth.

4. Cut along the lines and carefully push out the pieces.

5. Insert a plain white votive candle in a clear glass candle holder. *Remember: never leave a lit candle unsupervised.* Have a fire extinguisher readily available and see that everyone knows how to use it. Round, battery-powered touch-on lights available at most dollar stores also work great!

Pumpkin Preservation

Depending on weather conditions, a carved pumpkin can last anywhere from a day or two to more than a week. The best way to make a carved pumpkin last longer is to slow down the dehydration process and deter the onset of mold. Here are four ways to slow down the process:

Moisturize! When pumpkins shrivel, it's a sign that they are starting to dry up. You can usually restore them back to their original condition by soaking them in water overnight.

Oil it! Coat all cut surfaces of the pumpkin with petroleum jelly right after carving; lightly coat the interior as well. The petroleum jelly acts as a barrier that will help slow down the dehydration process. Use your finger to coat the eyes, nose, and mouth, and a jellied paper towel to coat the inside.

Keep it cool! Heat and direct sun will break down the pumpkin, so keep your jack-o-lantern in a dry, shaded area during the day. If you've got room in the fridge, keep it in there to slow down decomposition.

Preserve! A commercial spray-on preserver called Pumpkin Preserver is a cheap, environmentally friendly product that slows down the deterioration of pumpkins by deterring mold, rot, and bugs. It's made of all-natural ingredients and comes in a convenient spray bottle for easy application. Just spray the inside and cut surfaces lightly.

67

Puppy Chow for People

Kids and dogs are a natural mix. Maybe it's the built-in bond between two creatures who love to run and play. Even kids without a dog of their own seem to have a favorite dog, a stuffed animal, an animated creation, or a television or movie "star." For an afternoon of doggone fun, invite over several of your child's friends.

Guests can dine on peanut butter and jelly "dog bone" sandwiches, play Pin the Tail on the Puppy, and search for cardboard bones that can be redeemed for small prizes. Then sit everyone down to watch your child's favorite dog-themed movies (there are *lots* of them out there) while snacking on Puppy Chow for People.

To make the perfect puppy party snack, you'll need:

Corn or rice square cereal, 12 oz. box (11-12 cups)

1/2 cup butter or margarine

1-1/4 cups chocolate chips
3/4 cup smooth peanut butter
1-1/2 cups powdered sugar
A large mixing bowl
1 gallon zipper-top bag
A large saucepan

1. Measure the cereal into a large bowl. Set the bowl aside.

2. Pour the powdered sugar into a large zipper-top bag. Set the bag aside.

3. In a large saucepan, melt the butter and chocolate chips together over medium heat. Add the peanut butter. Stir constantly until the peanut butter is melted and the mixture is smooth.

4. Pour the mixture over the cereal, stir carefully so as not to break the cereal. Mix until all the cereal pieces are evenly coated.

5. Spoon half of the cereal mixture into the zipper-top bag with the powdered sugar. Seal and shake until all the cereal pieces are coated with powdered sugar. Add additional powdered sugar as necessary. Pour the coated treats onto a sheet of waxed paper to cool.

6. Repeat with the remainder of the cereal mixture. Store in an airtight container.

Doggie Dish

Once the puppy chow is made, your child can make a fun dish to serve it in. Start with a new, store-bought dog bowl (plastic, metal, or ceramic—your choice). Wash the bowl and dry it thoroughly. Using the correct primer, paint, and sealer for your type of bowl (for example, plastic paint and products for a plastic bowl, metal paint for a metal dish, and glass products for a ceramic crock), decorate the *outside* of the dish. Most of these nontoxic paints should not come into direct contact with food or drink. Let your decorated doggie dish dry completely before filling it with Puppy Chow for People.

68

Rainy Days

Hilo, Hawaii, is the rainiest city in the United States with an average of 129 inches falling there each year. If rainy days get you down no matter where you live, try turning those frowns upside down with these great rain-related projects. They're so much fun you might find yourself hoping it rains more often!

Rain Wear

Rainy days will seem much brighter to your child if she can decorate her own rain gear. You'll need a plain vinyl rain hat, coat, and rubber boots. Clean an area on the surface to be painted with rubbing alcohol. Let dry. Because all plastic paints are different, for best results, follow the manufacturer's recommendations for surface preparation, primer, painting, and sealing. Decorate with large polka dots, smiley faces, raindrops, rainbows, stick figures, curlicues, zigzags, hearts, stars, suns, or other favorite designs. If you have the time, patience, and talent, try turning a red pair of boots into ladybugs, a yellow pair into bumblebees, or maybe a blue pair into whales.

Raindrop Paintings

Once your rain wear is ready to go, slip it on and head out to create some art. Use washable markers to color simple shapes on a piece of white office paper. Your drawing can be as simple as a variety of long and short lines, circles, squares, and triangles. Don't invest a lot of time in an elaborate drawing, because you'll be using the rain to transform it into a new, unique piece of art. Take your drawing out on a day with light to moderate rain. Hold it flat, letting the rain hit your drawing for a minute or two. Lay the paper flat or hang it up to drip dry. Use the dried picture as stationery or wrapping paper, or frame it to hang on the wall.

Stay cool!

Keep a weather journal. In a small notebook, record information about the weather each day. Younger children can draw pictures representing the weather, while older kids can record highs and lows, amount of precipitation, averages, and forecasts. To estimate how far away the storm is (in miles): divide the number of seconds between the flash of lightening and the rumble of thunder by five. Also, next time the thunder and lightening keep you in, share *Thunder Cake* with your child—Patricia Polacco's wonderful tale of a Babushka (grandmother) helping a young girl overcome her fear of thunderstorms. Then bake a thunder cake of your own. Plan ahead so you'll have all the ingredients on hand before the storm hits.

69

A Rain Gauge

For many kids, a rainy day just means they can't go out and play their favorite games, but cool parents can turn a gray and rainy day into a fun science experiment. Kids can study many things about their own weather. The easiest way is to make a rain gauge and track the amount of rain you get in different storms or in different months of the year. Kids can learn more about the weather patterns in your area. Start by watching your local weather and discuss what kinds of things are happening in the atmosphere that affect your weather.

To make a rain gauge, you'll need:
A plastic ruler
Scissors
Clear, waterproof tape
Quart-sized jar with a wide mouth
A small notebook

1. Cut the ruler in half so that it will fit into the jar easily.

2. Tape the ruler in place inside the jar.

3. Place your jar in an open area where it can collect rain. Don't put the jar near a building or under trees.

4. After it rains, see how much rain actually fell. Try to measure to the nearest tenth of an inch.

5. Record the amount of rainfall you get for several rains, or keep track of rainfall for an entire month in your rainfall notebook.

6. To determine how much total rain you had for the month, add up all the measurements. See if the amount changes from one month or season to the next.

Stay cool!

If you've got a little weather forecasting fanatic at your house, see if you can arrange a visit to your local TV station to watch the meteorologist at work. If that's not possible, check out the following from your local library: *The Kids' Book of Weather Forecasting: Build a Weather Station, "Read" the Sky and Make Predictions!* by Mark Breen and Kathleen Friestad.

70

Rain Sticks

Rain storms are like nature's own laser light show. Before the performance even begins, the trees start to dance, swaying back and forth in the wind. Make some magical memories sitting outside on the grass watching a storm roll in. (Of course, you'll head inside when the lightning gets close or if conditions turn dangerous.) The first thing you'll see is flashes of lightning off in the distance followed closely by the sound of deep rumbles of thunder. As the storm gets closer, the lightning will be brighter and the thunder will get louder as the rain starts to fall, adding its own rhythmic melody. With a few supplies from your local office products store, you can reproduce that sound of the falling rain, even on the sunniest of days.

To make a magical rainmaker, you'll need:

Mailing tube (2 inches wide by 18 to 24 inches long) with end caps

1-inch finishing nails

Unpopped popcorn, rice, dried beans, or uncooked macaroni

White craft glue

Paper packing tape, Kraft paper tape, or any paper tape with a matte finish

Decorations such as stickers, markers, acrylic craft paint, and brushes or sponges

1. Remove both of the end caps on the tube. (If necessary, an adult should use a sharp kitchen knife to cut the tube to the desired length.)

2. Push nails into the sides of the tube, avoiding the seams. The more nails you insert, the more noise the rain stick will make.

3. When you think there are enough nails in the tube, put the bottom cap in place. Add about 1/2 cup of popcorn, rice, beans, macaroni, or some combination of these. Replace the top cap.

4. Hold the tube in a vertical position; rotate the tube upside down and back to right side up several times, making sure to hold the end caps in place. Change or add to the contents until you are happy with the sound your rain stick makes.

5. Remove the top cap, apply glue around the sides of the cap, and replace it. Allow the glue to set up, and then glue the other cap in place.

6. Wrap the tube with brown package tape.

7. Paint the tube as desired. Use additional paint, markers, and/or stickers to add additional decorations.

8. Allow the paint and the glue on the end caps to dry completely before using the rain stick.

71

Red, White, and Blue Desserts

Colorful Cake

You can turn an ordinary boxed cake mix into a perfectly patriotic dessert delight. Mix up a white cake mix according to the directions on the package. Divide the batter. Use food coloring to dye one half of the batter red and the other half blue. Bake in two round or square layer pans. Top with white frosting and decorate with stars cut from fruit roll treats.

Ice Cream Treat

For a cool treat on a hot night, whip up an ice cream delight with patriotic flair. Soften two cups vanilla ice cream, add several drops of blue food coloring, and pour the ice cream into a loaf pan that has been sprayed with non-stick spray. Freeze to harden. Repeat to add a white (vanilla) layer and a red (strawberry) layer. Slice and serve with blueberries, strawberries, and whipped topping, or scoop and serve in cones.

The Evening's Early Light

When it's time to serve your patriotic goodies, you and your child can light your table with these Americana-inspired candle holders.

You'll need:

Red, white, and blue tissue paper

White glue

Water

A paintbrush

A votive candleholder

1. Cut sheets of red, white, and blue tissue paper into small 1- to 2-inch squares.

2. Mix together equal parts white glue and water.

3. Brush the mixture onto one section of the votive candleholder.

4. Attach a tissue square to that section.

5. Repeat until the entire candleholder is covered.

6. Brush a coat of the glue mixture over the top of the tissue paper pieces and let dry.

72

Shrink-Plastic Tags

What would you do if you woke up one morning and you were just two inches tall? Pop a bowl of popcorn and spend some time pondering that question with your child. Lots of things would be fairly difficult. You wouldn't be able to reach *anything*, except maybe the dust bunnies under your bed. You would have to worry about being stepped on by everyone, including your pet hamster, who would be a giant compared to you. And even if you could walk around the house without fear of being stepped on, how long would it take you to get from your bedroom to the kitchen? Would there be anything good about being that small? See if your child can think up five benefits to being two inches tall.

After imagining, you can shrink a special art project to a fraction of its original size.

To make this miniature magic art, you'll need:

Computer clip art or coloring book pages for patterns*

Crafting shrink plastic

Sand paper (fine grit)

Permanent markers

Colored pencils

A hole puncher

Ball chain and ball chain connectors

Wire cutters

Note: *It's hard to make complicated cuts when working with shrink plastic. One way to solve this problem is to cut a simple shape such as a circle, square, triangle, or hexagon around your more intricate pattern.*

1. Use a photocopier or computer scanner to reduce or enlarge the pattern as needed. When preparing the pattern, keep in mind that shrink plastic generally shrinks forty to fifty percent of its original size.

2. Lightly sand one side of the shrink plastic in both directions: up-and-down and side-to-side.

3. Place the photocopied pattern underneath the plastic,

sanded side up. Trace the pattern onto the plastic with a permanent marker.

4. Decorate the item using colored pencils and permanent markers. The colors will intensify when the piece is shrunk.

5. Cut out the item. Use a hole puncher to put a hole in the top.

6. Shrink according to the manufacturer's directions on the package.

7. Attach a piece of ball chain three to four inches long.

73

Homemade Silly Putty

You can bounce it, squeeze it, even make copies of comic strips with it, and it hasn't shown any signs of going out of style. From its start in a scientist's lab in 1943, Silly Putty has become an American classic toy.

Scottish engineer James Wright was looking for a synthetic rubber compound at his General Electric lab in New Haven, when one day he combined boric acid and silicone oil to see what would happen. Removing the stuff from the test tube, he took a tentative bounce on the floor, and voila! Bouncing Putty was born. For several years the company tried in vain to come up with an industrial use for the rubbery stuff. Eventually, it was packed into little plastic eggs by marketing whiz Peter Hodgson, who named it Silly Putty and started showing it around. Sales were sluggish until a *New Yorker* writer published an article about the new toy that triggered a buying frenzy. Orders for 250,000 eggs poured in within three days. Soon, ads were appearing on the *Howdy Doody Show* and *Captain Kangaroo*, and a craze was born. More than 300 million eggs of the stuff have been produced since 1950. That's about 4,500 tons of the beige gunk!

Although the original was made with silicone, kids can make their own fun version right at home. All you need is two parts multi-purpose white glue and one part liquid starch. Make sure the label says "multi-purpose" because tacky craft glue or white school glue will *not* work. Mix the ingredients and let the mixture sit until it's workable. If the mixture is sticky, work in additional starch. Store in a zipper-top bag or airtight container. Note: This recipe might not work on humid days.

Stay cool!

Your kitchen can be a truly magical place when you use everyday household products to create really cool concoctions. Goodrich, Michigan, elementary teacher and science specialist Becky Ballance suggests checking out *Mad Professor: Concoct Extremely Weird Science Projects* by Mark Frauenfelder. She also recommends www.funology.com, which offers both online and print newsletters packed full of fun activities.

74

Snow Globes

Snow globes have been a vacation souvenir favorite for decades. Also called snow domes, snow scenes, and snow shakers, these cool collectibles are popular with children and adults alike. With a few supplies you can create miniature worlds based on your child's favorite things and maybe best of all, you can decide on any number of things to make it "snow."

To make one of these tiny treasures, you'll need:

A small glass baby food jar and lid (short/wide jars are better than tall/narrow ones)

Metal paint and brushes or sponges (optional)

Small plastic, resin, or other waterproof figurines

Nail polish remover

Waterproof glue

Baby oil or mineral oil

Non-metallic glitter

1. Wash the lid with warm, soapy water, and dry it well. If desired, paint the lid. Set the lid aside and allow the paint to dry completely.

2. Soak the jar in warm soapy water until you can easily remove the label. Use nail polish remover to remove any remaining adhesive and codes printed on the jar.

3. Glue the small plastic figurines to the underside of the lid. To add dimension to your scene, mound the glue in several spots. Allow the glue to set up slightly before inserting the figurine.

4. Allow the glue to dry completely. If you mounded the glue, it could take several days to dry completely.

5. Fill the jar about half full of baby oil or mineral oil. Put the lid on the jar to see how much oil is displaced by the figurines. Remove the lid and add additional oil until there is about 1/2 inch of air space when the lid is in place.

6. Add a small amount of "snow." Ultra-fine glitter gives an iridescent shimmer to the water, whereas large white glitter looks more like snow. Experiment with a variety of glitters, individually and several mixed together, until you get the effect you like. If you find some small plastic confetti that matches or complements your theme of figurines, add some to the mix.

7. Screw the lid into place and "test" the snow globe. Add additional snow until you are happy with the effect.

8. Make sure the lid is screwed on tightly. Run a line of glue between the bottom edge of the lid and the jar to seal the snow globe. Allow the glue to dry completely.

Stay cool!

As your child gets older, consider creating snow domes using collector quality kits with wooden bases and glass globes or domes.

75

Snowmen

Maybe it's all the tales that have been told, or maybe it's the glistening white powder used in their creation. Whatever the reason, most people agree that snowmen are special. If your child has any doubts, share with him *Snowmen at Night* by Caralyn and Mark Buehner. This delightful tale was inspired by the Buehner's own snowman experience, when the family awoke to find their snowman several yards from where they had built him. (And if that wasn't mysterious enough, the snowman was facing toward the house, instead of away from it as it had been the night before.)

You never know what fun will happen when you build a snowman, so be ready before the next snowfall! Gather up your kids and have a ball making your own "snowman kit."

To make this wintertime wonder, you'll need:

2 large rocks, 2 to 3 inches in diameter

6 to 8 small rocks, about 1 inch in diameter

Artificial carrot (plastic or wood) 5 to 6 inches long

1/4 yard fleece fabric
1/4-inch dowel, 8 inches long
Knit hat
Black acrylic craft paint and brushes or sponges
Heavy-duty, all-purpose waterproof glue
Drill with 1/4-inch bit

1. To make the eyes, paint the two large rocks black or the color of your choice.

2. For the nose, drill a hole in the center of the flat end of the carrot. If you're using a solid carrot, drill about 2 inches into the carrot. (If you can't find an artificial carrot, use polymer clay to create a carrot.) Follow the manufacturer's recommendations for finishing and sealing.

3. Using waterproof glue, glue the dowel into the carrot.

4. For the mouth, paint the small rocks.

5. For the scarf, cut a strip of fleece about 6 inches wide and 36 to 45 inches long. If desired, cut fringe or zigzag the ends of the scarf.

6. Collect mittens or gloves, a pipe, and other accessories for your snowman.

Stay cool!

Once it snows and you've built your snowman, head inside and work together with your child to write and illustrate your own version of what your snowman might do at night in your neighborhood or town.

76

Snowy Snowman Mints

While snowmen may indeed be magical creations, not everyone is fortunate enough to be able to create one. In fact, even those people who do live in snowy areas are often at the mercy of Mother Nature, who ultimately decides if and when there will be enough snow to decorate the front and/or back yard with the roly-poly "people."

A fun alternative that everyone can make any time the mood strikes are these *edible* miniature snowy snowman mints.

To make these melt-in-your-mouth snowmen, you'll need:

1/2 cup butter, softened

1/4 cup cream

6 cups powdered sugar

Mint extract or flavoring

Food coloring
Waxed paper
A mixing bowl

1. In a bowl, mix together softened butter and cream.

2. Gradually add powdered sugar.

3. Add mint extract or flavoring to taste.

4. Knead with hands when dough is too stiff to stir.

5. With three-fourths of the dough, form small bits of dough into balls about the size of marbles. Stack the balls two high and place them on waxed paper to dry.

6. Tint the remaining dough with food coloring. Make little hats and scarves for snowmen.

7. Decorate snowmen with sprinkles for mouth, eyes, nose, and buttons. Dust with additional powdered sugar if desired. Store in the refrigerator in an airtight container.

77

Homemade Soap with a Surprise

Parents sometimes have a pretty tough time getting their children into the tub for a bath. Toss in a bar of soap with a toy surprise in the center and you'll have a tough time getting them *out* of the tub! Kids of all ages will love this brightly-colored, surprise-filled soap. It not only makes bath time and hand washing lots of fun, but it makes a great gift or party favor, so make extras. Best of all, it's quick, easy, and fun.

To make your own surprise soap, you'll need:

A sharp kitchen knife (adult use only)

Clear glycerin soap (sometimes called pour-and-melt soap base)

A large, microwave-safe glass measuring cup

Soap dye or colorant (optional)

A soap mold or small disposable margarine container (large enough to hold a toy)

Small plastic or waterproof toys
A toothpick or craft stick
Non-stick cooking spray

1. Lightly spray the soap mold or margarine container with non-stick cooking spray. Use a paper towel to wipe off any excess oil. Set the container aside.

2. Cut the glycerin into 1-inch cubes. Put several of the cubes into the measuring cup. CAUTION: Glycerin is flammable, so an adult should monitor the microwave closely while it melts.

3. Microwave the soap chunks for about 15 seconds at a time, stirring in between. *Do not melt the chunks completely.* When most of the chunks are melted, remove from the microwave and stir until any remaining pieces melt.

4. Stir in a couple of drops of soap dye or color, if desired.

5. Pour a layer of soap (about 1/2 to 3/4 inch thick) into the mold.

6. Let the soap harden (about 10 to 15 minutes).

7. Place the toy face down on the hardened soap.

8. Melt a few more cubes of soap, add color if desired. For a little extra fun, make the soap two-toned by using different

colors for the top and bottom layers. Carefully pour another layer, 1/2- to 3/4-inch thick (or until the toy is completely covered). If the toy starts to rise as the second layer of soap is poured, use a toothpick or craft stick to push it back down and hold it in place for a few seconds.

9. Let the soap harden completely before removing it from the mold. If the soap will not release from the mold, place the mold in the freezer for about 30 minutes.

78

Spray-Painted Shirts

Anyone who's ever tried tie-dying knows what fun it is, but also what a mess it can be. This alternative way to colorize a shirt, with all the fun and none of the mess, is sure to be a hit at your house.

And there's no need to stop with shirts! When you're finished with the T-shirts, use the leftover paint mixture to spray prewashed sheets, towels, pillowcases, socks, or canvas tennis shoes.

To make your own colorful creations, you'll need:

1 cup warm water

A white cotton T-shirt

A large piece of heavy cardboard, cut to fit inside the T-shirt

Acrylic craft paint

Empty plastic jars with lids, washed

Small squirt bottles, one per color

Doilies, miscellaneous die cuts, and/or stencils (optional)
A fabric softener sheet

1. Wash and dry the shirt *without* fabric softener.

2. Put 1 cup warm tap water and a couple of tablespoons of paint in a jar. Screw the lid on tightly, and shake the jar until the water and paint are mixed. The mixture should look like colored water. To get dark, more vibrant colors, use a higher concentration of paint.

3. Pour the mixture into a squirt bottle.

4. Repeat for each color.

5. Insert a piece of cardboard (cut to fit) inside each shirt.

6. Lay the shirt outside on the grass or on a piece of newspaper.

7. Arrange doilies, die cuts, or shapes cut from cardboard on the shirt.

8. Spray a color on the shirt.

9. Move or remove the die cuts or other shapes and spray another color. Repeat until the desired effect is achieved.

10. Let the shirt air-dry for 15 to 30 minutes, or until the shirt is just slightly damp.

11. Finish drying the shirt in the dryer on medium heat with a fabric softener sheet. If you completely air-dry the shirt, it may feel somewhat stiff. The stiffness will disappear once the shirt has been washed and machine dried.

Stay cool!

Use a variety of pastel shades to create colorful and fun baby T-shirts and onesies. Donate the shirts to your local pregnancy services or crisis center, or other community service agency for distribution to families in need. Hospitals often keep some baby clothes on hand to help parents faced with the prospect of taking their child home in nothing but a diaper.

79

Stained Glass Candy

Stained glass windows adorn the walls of many churches and even a number of public buildings such as the courthouse, city hall, or public services building. Sometimes the windows tell a story: in a church it may be a religious story, or in a government building the window might tell the tale of the area's early settlers, display the crest of the city, or feature the emblem of the police or fire department.

These works of art are made from large sheets of colored and textured glass cut into hundreds or thousands of pieces for each design. Then the window is carefully assembled, just like a large jigsaw puzzle.

While your child may not be old enough to tackle these creations just yet, you can work together to make sheets of candy that resemble the materials used in real stained glass windows.

To make this edible "glass," you'll need:

3/4 cup light corn syrup

2 cups sugar

1 cup water

Flavored oil (for best results, choose a flavor that is colorless or lightly colored)

Liquid food coloring

A candy thermometer

A large saucepan

A large jellyroll pan

A toothpick or skewer

1. Mix the corn syrup, sugar, and water together in a large saucepan. Affix the candy thermometer inside the pan.

2. Cook over medium heat, stirring occasionally, until the mixture reaches 300°F/149°C (hard crack consistency) on the candy thermometer.

3. Remove the pan from the heat and stir in 1/4 teaspoon flavored oil.

4. Carefully pour the mixture into a large jellyroll pan. Be very careful, as the mixture will be very hot.

5. Immediately place drops of food coloring using one or

more colors on the surface of the candy in various spots. Using a toothpick or skewer, swirl the color throughout the candy. This step must be done quickly, because the candy will start to harden as soon as it is poured into the pan.

6. Let the candy cool. Break it into small pieces and store the candy in an airtight container.

For Younger Kids

Children too young to help make sheets of stained glass candy can make colorful sun catchers of their own. Photocopy a coloring-book picture onto a sheet of transparency film. Most copy stores can do this for you. Your child can then color the picture using permanent markers. When the piece is dry, you or your child can cut around the design. Use a hole puncher to make holes in the top corners of the picture. Hang the sun catcher in the window using suction cups with hangers.

80

Star Spangled Tees

Foster national pride in your child with this fun red, white, and blue T-shirt project. Perfect for Memorial Day, Flag Day, July 4th, or any day, these shirts will be the hit of the holiday. It's simpler than you think to make one for every member of the family.

You'll need:
A white T-shirt
Contact paper
Masking tape
Cardboard
Fabric paint or acrylic paint with textile/fabric medium

1. Wash and dry white T-shirts *without* fabric softener.

2. Cut small star shapes out of contact paper.

3. Tape off a large rectangle on the front of the shirt.

4. Tape off a square in the upper left corner of the rectangle.

5. Arrange the stars in the square and adhere them to the shirt.

6. Tape off stripes in the remainder of the rectangle.

7. Insert a piece of cardboard inside the shirt.

8. With brushable fabric paint, or acrylic craft paint mixed with textile/fabric medium, paint the square blue, and every other stripe red.

9. Remove the stars and tape before the paint has completely dried. Allow the shirt to dry and heat-set according to the paint manufacturer's instructions.

81

Star Treatment

Every kid is a star, or at least a star-in-training. He may not be the next *American Idol* or she may not be a top athlete, but in the eyes of their parents and teachers, every child has the potential to be a shining star. Part of the fun (and sometimes the frustration) of being a parent or mentor is helping a child find the talent that will make her shine by celebrating the accomplishments, consoling the failures, and giving her "star treatment" throughout it all. Let your budding star know how proud you are of her with one or more of these fun ideas.

Trading Cards

Every sports superstar has her picture on a trading card. Why not make trading cards starring your child? Don't reserve this project for the athletically inclined; you can personalize your child's cards to match her talents and interests. Purchase a package of name badges designed for your home computer/printer from your local office-supply store. Using a desktop publishing program's template for the badges you bought, on the front of the card, insert a digital picture of your child along with her name and theme-related clip-art. Alternatively, you can paste a photo on the card and draw your own theme-related art. On the back of the badge, print fun information about your child, including: her favorite color, favorite food, and a personal quote. Laminate the cards for lasting entertainment.

With the help and input of your child, you could make a whole pack for all her friends and distribute them as party favors at your next birthday party!

RSVP

Let your child know the importance of that soccer game, dance recital, school assembly, or Scout ceremony by inviting family and friends to attend. Create theme-related invitations to announce the event. Don't reserve invitations for only the special events or play-off games. Instead, invite people to regular season games or even practices so they can see your star in action!

Home Show

How do you share your child's talent if she pursues a hobby or interest by herself outside of school? What if your child is a tal-ented self-taught artist, a photographer or videographer, or takes private music lessons? Hold an exhibit, showing, or recital to show-case your child's talent and hard work. Send formal invitations to family and friends. Display your child's art or plan for a short performance, serve cake and punch or fancy finger foods, and let your child shine.

And the Award Goes to...

Let your child know that you think he is a star even if he doesn't bring home an award. Purchase a small trophy and present it to your child for all his hard work.

Stay cool!
Plan an afternoon at the planetarium and check out some *real* superstars.

82

Make Your Own Stickers

Young children and their friends love being showered with cool stickers; many younger kids can invest several hours in filling up their sticker books. Buying stickers, however, can quickly become expensive, especially if you have several children to entertain.

Here's a fun activity to do together than can make stickering a memorable family craft activity.

To make your own stickers, you'll need:

1 packet (1/4 ounce) unflavored gelatin

1 tbsp. cold water

3 tbsp. boiling water

1/2 tsp. white corn syrup or sugar

1/2 tsp. lemon or vanilla extract

A sheet of paper with small drawings or pictures

1. In a small bowl, sprinkle the gelatin into cold water.

2. Let the gelatin sit for five minutes. Pour boiling water into the soft gelatin and stir it until it's dissolved.

3. Add the corn syrup or sugar and the vanilla extract. Mix this well to form a brushable gum substance.

4. Choose the design for your stickers. Draw small pictures on an 8 x 11-inch piece of paper, reduce favorite photos on a color copier, or choose pictures in a magazine or book.

5. Brush the gum thinly on the back of the paper. Cover the entire sheet.

6. Allow the page to dry completely. The paper will curl up as it dries.

7. Press the page under something heavy (such as the phone book) to flatten it.

8. Cut out the stickers. You can either cut a simple square with the design inside, or follow the lines of the design.

9. Moisten the sticker and apply to paper.

83

Stone Soup

The classic story of "stone soup" has been told for centuries. No matter where the story takes place, the premise is always the same: A hungry traveler (sometimes more than one) with nothing to eat uses a pot of boiling water and a stone to trick the townsfolk into helping him cook a delicious pot of soup. This magical tale shows children the benefits of sharing and working together.

After reading this tale with your child, invite several friends over for a simple dinner of "stone soup." When planning this meal, figure at least twelve to sixteen ounces for each adult and six to eight ounces for each child.

To make a pot of this storybook cuisine, you'll need:

A large stone*, the size of a potato

Vegetable juice

Fresh vegetables, including potatoes, carrots, celery, and onions

Canned vegetables, including diced tomatoes, cut green beans, peas, and whole kernel corn

Rice, egg noodles, or small pasta noodles

A large stockpot

* Note: *about stones: For best results, Central Michigan University geology professor Reed Wicander suggests choosing a dense rock such as quartzite, limestone, or marble. He recommends avoiding any red rock, which contains iron; shale, which would break apart during cooking; or any rock with "flakes" that might shed during cooking.*

1. Wash the rock with hot, soapy water. Use a brush to scrub any dirt and debris out of the crevices of the rock and boil the rock in a pan of water to kill germs.

2. Put the rock into a large stockpot. Add equal parts vegetable juice and water. Warm over medium heat.

3. Wash the fresh vegetables and dice them.

4. Add the veggies to the pot. Heat the mixture on high until it boils, then reduce the heat to low. Simmer about 30 minutes, or until the potatoes and carrots are soft.

5. Drain the canned vegetables, except for the tomatoes. Add to the soup and simmer for 15 minutes.

6. Add rice or pasta (2 to 4 tablespoons per person) and simmer for another 15 minutes or until cooked.

7. Salt and pepper to taste.

Stay cool!

For a true "Stone Soup" experience, invite each child guest to contribute one type of fresh or canned vegetable. As host, your child provides the vegetable juice and the stone. When everyone arrives, add your stone, and let guests add their contributions one by one. Share your favorite version of the "Stone Soup" story with dinner guests while the pot of stone soup simmers.

84

Stories

Bedtime stories are a part of the evening ritual in many homes with small children. It's a wonderful way to settle down after a busy day and share information about faraway places, fantastic tall tales, or the latest adventures of a favorite character. Some families continue this tradition as the children read through longer works one chapter at a time. Some of these books become favorites, and some you'll read to your child over and over.

Think of the wonderful memories your child can create by writing her own bedtime stories. With a few "story starters," it can be easier than you think to inspire a masterpiece.

Story Circle

This activity works best with a group of people. Everyone sits in a circle and someone starts a story. For young children, adults may need to provide the bulk of the story, leaving the fun details for the children to fill in. For example, an adult might start: "Once upon a time there was a giraffe named..." setting up for a response from a child. Another adult might add: "His favorite food wasn't leaves, it was..." to which a child could supply a funny food. The story would continue in this way until reaching a conclusion.

For older children, let each person in the circle add one or two words at a time building on to the story as it travels around the circle. As you play this game, be sure to have a tape recorder running. That way, you can transcribe the story and add illustrations.

A Page at a Time

On the first page of a spiral-bound notebook, write the opening paragraphs of a story. Leave the book with a supply of writing utensils in a place accessible to the whole family. Encourage everyone to add a paragraph or two as they have ideas. Younger children can dictate their contributions to a parent or an older sibling, or provide illustrations. When the story is complete, celebrate with a "book-reading party."

Story Cards

Use colored 5 x 7-inch index cards to create a set of story cards for your budding author. Write the words in large print and add pictures for the young readers and writers. On red cards, put different types of animals. On yellow cards, put action words (runs, eats, sleeps, jumps). On green cards, put adjectives (big, fast, blue). On blue cards, put places (house, school, grocery store). On white cards, put things (car, telephone, coat). Have your child pick one card of each color. Younger children can "write" a sentence with the cards, while older children can use them as elements in a story.

Stay cool!

Record your child's stories using archival quality supplies (paper, pens, and colored pencils for the illustrations), or have the originals copied onto acid-free paper. Store the pages in archival or scrapbook quality protectors and binders. With a little extra effort you can preserve your child's stories for his children to read someday.

85

Sunshine

According to *The Weather Almanac*, Yuma, Arizona, is the sunniest city in the United States. Residents there enjoy sunshine ninety percent of the year. Some of the other super-sunny U.S. cities are Redding, California; Las Vegas; Tucson; Phoenix; and El Paso.

But you don't have to live in one of these hot spots to enjoy the rays. Make the most of every sunny day, even if you live in Quillayute, Washington, the cloudiest city in the United States!

Super Shades

Get ready for the sunshine of summer by creating a pair of super-cool sunglasses. Use heavy-duty waterproof glue (such as E6000 or Goop) to glue a variety of small, flat objects like beads, flat buttons, wiggle eyes, foam cutouts, charms, small pom-poms, and/or faux gemstones to a pair of plastic sunglasses. Allow to dry completely before wearing. Decorate a pair for every member of the family, Mom and Dad included.

Sun Prints

Use the sun and a variety of household objects to create one-of-a-kind prints. You'll need to plan ahead, because this project requires light- or sun-sensitive paper, generally available at education stores, science-themed stores, and some museum shops. In a pinch, you can substitute construction paper, but the prints will fade over time. Collect a variety of uniquely shaped objects from around the house. Arrange the objects on the paper, creating an interesting pattern or design. Follow the manufacturer's suggestions for how long to leave your paper in the sun and information about rinsing the paper with water when you are done.

"Sun'Mores"

Line a large metal bowl with aluminum foil, with the shiny side facing you. Place the bowl in a sunny spot for several hours. Once the bowl is nice and hot, put a marshmallow or two on a long stick, and hold them in the bowl until they are cooked. (Be careful not to touch the bowl!) When the marshmallows are done, sandwich them with chocolate pieces between two graham crackers for a new twist on a favorite campfire treat, without the campfire!

Stay cool!

Celebrate the first day of summer with a backyard barbecue. If Mother Nature cooperates, this will be the day with the longest sunlight. Spend the evening compiling a list of 101 things you'd like to do over the summer: books to read, places to go, crafts to make, and maybe even a list of ice cream flavors to try. Check off the items as you complete them.

86

Super Simple Cookies

Most parents believe that baking cookies is a memorable activity that kids can share with a parent, grandparent, or older friend. Unfortunately, today's busy families don't always have time to bake cookies from scratch. When you do find the time, it seems as if you never have all the necessary ingredients on hand.

But a cookie recipe with only three main ingredients is a cool idea! These cookies are so quick and so delicious, don't be surprised if you and your child start making homemade cookies more often!

To make these simply scrumptious, super simple cookies, you'll need:

2 eggs

2 cups sugar (white or brown, or a combination of the two)

2 cups peanut butter, creamy or chunky

1/2 cup chocolate chips or chopped peanuts (optional)

1/2 cup chocolate chips or Hershey Kisses (optional)
A large mixing bowl

1. Preheat the oven to 350°F.

2. In a large bowl, mix together the eggs and sugar.

3. Add the peanut butter and stir until completely mixed.

4. Add the chocolate chips or chopped peanuts (or both).

5. Roll into walnut-sized balls and place on cookie sheets. Flatten with a fork, making a crisscross on the top of each cookie.

6. Bake for 8 to 12 minutes, until lightly browned.

7. Remove from the oven. Place a chocolate piece or kiss into the center of each cookie if desired.

8. Let the cookies cool on the cookie sheet for 2 to 3 minutes. Remove to a cooling rack and let cool completely.

Stay cool!

Read *If You Give a Mouse a Cookie* by Laura Joffe Numeroff while sharing a batch of warm-from-the-oven cookies with your child.

87

Surprise Gift Balls

If it seems as if your kids fly through their presents on birthdays, Christmas, or Hanukkah, here's a wonderful way to slow them down a bit: a holiday ball of yarn with hidden surprises along the way! For this idea, you'll need a ball of yarn with thick, soft strands and lots of tiny toys like stickers, tiny notebooks, little dolls, small candies, and so on.

Version I

Begin making your Surprise Gift Ball by wrapping a few strands of wool around the first little toy. As you continue wrapping, add another toy every few layers until the ball is as big as your child can comfortably handle. As your child slowly unwraps the ball, she'll discover each tiny toy.

Version II

If you have larger gifts that won't fit into a ball, you can have your child follow a yarn trail from one room throughout the house, up chairs and over tables, in and out of closets, finding presents along the way. The yarn trail should end back where he started, where the biggest surprise awaits his return.

88

Sweet Dreams

One of the first milestones that most new parents find themselves dreaming about is getting their child to sleep through the night. Those peaceful nights often disappear again around the toddler years, when nightmares, scary shadows, or monsters under the bed keep your child awake. Help your child spend a little more time in that sweet place called "dreamland" with these activities designed to promote good dreams and ward off monsters.

Catching Dreams

You can make your own "dream catcher" from a kit available at most craft stores. Dream catchers appear in many Native American cultures, where it is believed that dreams are trapped in the web. The good dreams travel down the feather to the person sleeping below, while the bad dreams remain trapped in the web. When the morning sun hits the dream catcher, the bad dreams are burned up. Dream catchers were originally made from willow branches and sinew. Today's dream catchers often incorporate other materials, which can be bought in many gift or craft shops.

No More Monsters

It seems that no matter what Mom or Dad does, monsters come crawling out from the closets and under the bed. Help your child ward off any creepy creatures that might inhabit his room by mixing up a batch of monster repellent. Decorate a small spray bottle with water and a pinch or two of ultra-fine glitter (magic anti-monster dust). Label the bottle. Each night before your child goes to bed, help him spray under the bed, in the closet, in the corners, and any place else that monsters lurk. Repeat as necessary.

Another way to keep the monsters at bay is to get them on your side. Purchase or make a friendly-looking, stuffed "good" monster. Position the monster in your child's room to act as a guard who will keep all the bad monsters away.

"Bad Dream Buster" Box

If it's bad dreams and not monsters that plague your child's slumber, try banishing those nightmares to a special "bad-dream buster" box.

You'll need:

A small cardboard or wooden box

Stickers of happy things (smiley faces, rainbows, fairies, stars, or balloons)

Dimensional craft paint or glue

Glitter
A notebook and pencil

1. Decorate a small cardboard or wooden box with pictures or stickers.

2. Use dimensional craft paint or glue and glitter to add some extra touches.

3. If your child is old enough, stock the box with a small notepad and pencil. For younger children, keep the pad and pencil someplace you can grab it quickly on the way to comfort your child.

4. When the child wakes up from a bad dream, write down a few key words to represent the dream and place the paper into the box.

5. If possible, remove the note before your child wakes up in the morning, leaving behind a sprinkling of glitter and maybe a special note of encouragement.

89

An Old-Fashioned Taffy Pull

Long before the advent of videos, computer games, and digital entertainment, kids still found ways to have fun together. Gathering at a friend's house for a session of songs and taffy pulling or fudge-making was one favorite pastime. The next time you're faced with a houseful of kids, head to the kitchen for some old-time taffy-pulling.

To make taffy, you'll need:

2 cups light corn syrup

2 cups sugar

2/3 cup water

1/4 tsp. salt

Flavoring extracts or oils

Food coloring (optional)

Butter

A candy thermometer
A jellyroll pan
A saucepan

1. Butter a jellyroll pan. Set the pan aside.

2. Combine ingredients in saucepan and boil on medium heat to 250°F/121°C (hard ball consistency) on the candy thermometer.

3. Pour the mixture into the buttered pan and let it rest until it's cool enough to handle.

4. Butter your hands and take a lump of taffy. Pull and stretch it until it is light and slightly firm. (The longer the candy is pulled the more air it will have, and the better it will taste.)

5. Stretch the taffy out into a rope and cut the pulled taffy into bite-sized pieces with scissors.

6. When the taffy is completely cool, wrap it in waxed paper or colored plastic wrap.

7. Try different flavors of taffy by adding flavored extract to taste: mint, butterscotch, vanilla, raspberry, or root beer.

Stay cool!

If your kids enjoyed going "back in time" in the kitchen, they might like to find out about some more old-fashioned fun. Share with them some of the books in the *Betsy-Tacy* series, by Maud Hart Lovelace, that traces the friendship of two girls from early childhood through marriage in a small Minnesota town of the early 1900s.

90

Tangrams—An Ancient Puzzle

According to legend, the first tangram puzzle was created in China more than a thousand years ago when a porcelain tile was dropped, breaking into seven pieces—two large triangles, one medium triangle, two small triangles, a square, and a parallelogram. While trying to assemble the pieces back into a square, it was discovered that numerous designs (known as tangrams) could be created. In proper tangrams, all seven pieces, called "tans," are used, and the pieces are connected at their sides or edges, not their corners.

This puzzle is so popular that a number of books have been published featuring pictures of objects that have been created with the seven pieces. Encourage your child to be creative and make what they see in the pieces. Challenge older children to assemble the square. Work together and see what you can create: people, animals, cars, houses, and letters of the alphabet. For young fans of *Sagwa, The Chinese Siamese Cat*, the PBS website (http://pbskids.org/sagwa/games/tangrams/index.html) features an interactive tangram game in which visitors can try to build Sagwa, Fu-Fu, Mama Miao, Tai Tai, the Reader, the Magistrate, along with other characters and show-related items.

To make a tangram puzzle for your child, simply transfer the pattern (see below) to a piece of cardboard or craft foam and cut out the pieces. Tangrams are the perfect portable puzzle. Keep a set for each child on hand; you can store the precut pieces in small zipper-top bags and take them along whenever you head out. It's a great activity when you're waiting for dinner in a restaurant, when the dentist is running late, or any time you have access to a flat surface to work on. To fight backseat boredom, cut a tangram set out of magnetic sheeting and give each child a cookie sheet for a work surface.

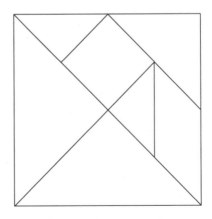

91

Terrific Timepieces

For most families with children, some days it seems like the clock is running your lives; work, meetings, appointments, errands, soccer practice, and dance lessons all require you to stay on schedule. If you fall behind, it throws off the rest of the day. It's no wonder that watches and clocks are such a vital part of the day-to-day routine. Even children as young as preschool pick up the importance of time and want to learn how to read an analog clock.

With an inexpensive clock movement from your local craft store you can create a fun, one-of-a-kind timepiece that will make staying on time a joy. And best of all, making one is so quick and so simple that you can make one for every room of the house or each member of the family.

Clock Body

Predrilled wooden clock forms in a variety of shapes and sizes are readily available. But you can use just about anything for your clock body, the possibilities are limitless. The only two things to keep in mind when selecting your clock box is that you need to be able to put a hole in it, and its sides shouldn't be thicker than 3/4 inch. Other than that, anything goes!

Foam core board is a good material. It's inexpensive, readily available, and can easily be cut into any shape imaginable. Also, decorations such as craft foam, pictures, fabric can be mounted to the foam core board.

You can even use a cereal box or snack box to make your clock body. Carefully open the box along the seam and glue a piece of foam core board to the front of the box (on the inside) for stability. Perhaps, you'd like to video box clock, using the plastic box from a favorite video. Or if you have access to a masonry drill bit, consider using a plate or ceramic tile as the clock face. Be creative. If you decide to make a cereal box clock, make sure you can reach the battery to change it after the box has been reassembled. Also, you may need to add a zipper-top bag filled with sand or rice in the bottom for stability.

Face Decorations

Use anything to decorate the face of the clock. Some great options are stickers, flat buttons, coins, charms, beads, craft foam cutouts, or small wood cutouts. Paint or embellish the face with permanent markers. Some computer craft programs even have clock faces that you can use.

Putting It All Together

Follow the manufacturer's directions for assembling and installing the clock movement. For wall mounting, secure a hanger to the back of the clock or attach a plate hanger. You can also display the clock on a plate stand.

92

Tin Can Night Lights

Fireflies, twinkling stars, and the moon are all able to brighten the darkness of an otherwise dark and scary nighttime sky. With a trip to the recycling bin and a little help from you, your child can create a set of lanterns to brighten and add a hint of magic along your driveway or the walk to your house. So simple and fun, you might want to create a new set for each holiday or season. For safety reasons, use the lanterns outdoors only.

To get started, you'll need:

Large tin cans, washed and dried (coffee cans work very well)

Common nails, 1-1/2 inches long

A hammer

Simple patterns like stars, snowflakes, crescent moons, or letters
(spell out a word, or maybe even your surname)

Masking tape

A large bath towel
Spray paint (optional)
Sand or cat litter
Votive candles
Water to fill the cans

1. Fill the cans with water and freeze the water in a freezer, or outside if the weather is cold enough.

2. Once the can is frozen, use masking tape to attach the patterns to the can.

3. Lay the can on its side on top of a folded bath towel to keep it from rolling.

4. Use a hammer and a nail to carefully tap holes into the can, following the pattern and creating a line of holes with a space a half-inch along the outline of the pattern.

5. Place the can in the sink until the water inside the can melts. Dump any remaining water from the can, and dry the can completely.

6. Spray the outside of the can with acrylic paint. Let the paint dry completely.

7. Fill the bottom of the can with 1 to 2 inches of sand or cat litter for stability. Set a candle in the center of the can.

93

Make-Your-Own Toy Train

Your little train fanatic will get miles of fun out of this toy train made from empty juice boxes and thread spools.

To make your own train, you'll need:

4 (4 to 7 oz.) juice boxes of different sizes
String or twine
10 empty thread spools
Single hole puncher
White craft glue

1. Wash and dry the empty juice boxes.

2. On the top and bottom panels, pull down one triangle flap on the same side and punch a hole through it.

3. Cut the string into 2-inch segments and tie the boxes together so they are about one inch apart.

4. To make this a pull toy, leave about 8 to 10 inches of extra string at the front.

5. Glue two spools under each box for the wheels.

6. Glue a smaller spool on top of the first box as the smoke stack.

7. Glue another small spool on the front to create the cow-catcher.

8. Paint or decorate the outside of the boxes.

Stay cool!

If you live near a train station, consider taking the family on a short train trip, just for the experience. Or curl up with a train-related book, such as *Terrific Trains* by Tony Mitton.

94

Tricky Pictures

Magic tricks, puzzles, riddles, and optical illusions mystify and amaze kids of all ages. And they are so proud when they figure out or solve them. Help your kids create tricky, optical illusion photographs that will delight their friends. Creating an optical illusion is actually very simple; once you get the hang of it, you and your kids will be able to create your own, one-of-a-kind tricky pictures. If you have access to a digital camera, consider using it to take your pictures. You will be able to tell immediately if you have things positioned correctly to create the desired illusion.

The Human Octopus

This is a fun tricky picture for two or more friends. Dressed in identical tops, arrange the friends so that the smaller person is in the back, but with arms extended so they are visible. Have the back person crouch down a bit so that his arms are *slightly* lower than the person in front. Give each person two things to hold; experiment with things such as pom-poms, tennis rackets, footballs, or basketballs. Now take the photo of one person with four arms!

Experiment with three friends for a total of six arms, or four friends and eight arms.

Extreme Close-Up

Fool your friends with cool close-up shots of everyday items. As you take these pictures, try to avoid capturing background items that may distract from the shot or provide clues to the identity of the object. Half the fun of taking these pictures is deciding what objects to use. Try shooting extreme close-ups of a sponge, an orange, a bowl of dried beans, pasta, or rice, a comb or brush, a soccer ball, a part of your pet, grass, or anything that you think would make an interesting picture.

Do You See What I See?

These pictures will take some time to put together, but they are worth the effort. On a large surface such as a piece of poster board, lay lots of small items. For example, you might arrange a hundred pennies, placing all but one facing up. Or you might arrange flat buttons of different shapes, with only one star button in the group. Take the picture from directly above the surface, getting as close as you can and still get the whole shot. Challenge your friends to find the wrong penny, the star button, or whatever item that you have planted in your picture.

95

Tumbling Blocks (Jacob's Ladder)

With all the toys and diversions available, it's comforting to know that a simple toy made from wooden blocks and ribbon still enchants children. Tumbling blocks have a rich history. According to legend, a set of tumbling blocks was buried with King Tut—that would make this toy more than three thousand years old! These blocks are also sometimes called Jacob's Ladder, named for the Bible story in which Jacob has a vision of a ladder reaching from earth to heaven.

To make a set of these amazing tumbling blocks, you'll need:

A piece of soft wood (pine or poplar) 1/2-inch thick, 2 inches wide, and at least 2 ft. long

A hand saw or power saw (adult use only)

Sandpaper

Acrylic craft paint and brushes (optional)

1/2-inch grosgrain ribbon: 1 yard of one color (Ribbon A) and 2 yards of another color (Ribbon B)

Carpet tacks

A hammer

A pencil

1. Cut the wood into six or more blocks measuring 2 inches wide by 3 inches long.

2. Sand all surfaces until smooth.

3. Paint the blocks in all the same color or a variety of colors.

4. Stand each block on an end that you cut, and mark the center on the top of the block with a pencil.

5. Tack one end of Ribbon A into the point that you marked.

6. Cut Ribbon B in half.

7. Tack the end of one length of Ribbon B into the opposite end of the block about 1/4 inch from the outer edge. Tack the other length of Ribbon B next about 1-3/4 from the edge. There should be about 1 inch between the tacked ends of the two lengths of Ribbon B.

8. Lay the block flat and pull all the ribbons across the block

so that the end of Ribbon A and the ends of Ribbon B are at opposite ends.

9. Set a second block on top of the first block. Bring the center ribbon around the edge and down the center of this second block. Tack the ribbon in place on the end of the block—the opposite end from where it is tacked on the first block. Repeat with the other two ribbons; bring each around the end of block two and down the side, tack in place. Don't pull the ribbons tight or the blocks won't tumble when you are finished.

10. Continue this pattern with the remaining blocks.

11. Clip off any excess ribbon. When you stand your finished stack on end, you should have an alternating pattern of ribbons.

12. Hold the end two blocks in your hand, letting the rest fall into a column. Let go of the outer block (the one directly above the column) and watch the blocks tumble.

13. Check the blocks occasionally for loose tacks that need to be tapped back into place. If needed, use a drop of super-glue to help hold the ribbon and tack in place.

Top view of block #1, ribbons in place. Fasten the ribbons on the edge of the block.

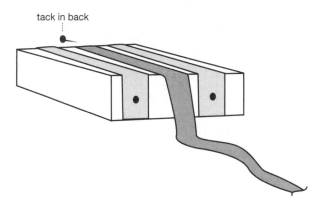

tack in back

Top view of block #2, ribbons in place, stacked on top of block #1. Wrap the ribbon around the edge of the block #2 and tack in place.

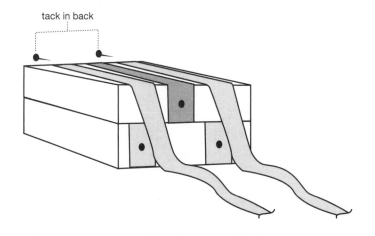

tack in back

Top view of block #3, ribbons in place, stacked on top blocks #1 and #2.

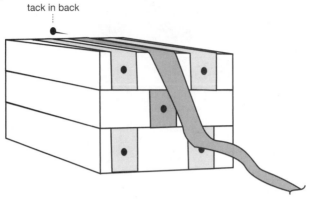

tack in back

Vertical view of a five block Jacob's Ladder. Your ladder may differ slightly; it may appear backwards or upside-down, depending on how you are holding it.

96

Make-Your-Own Watercolor Paints

Any parent who has ever stared at a blank piece of paper before a looming deadline knows how daunting it can be. In the hands of a child, that same sheet of blank paper has the potential to become anything: folded into a paper crane, a note to a friend, part of a homework assignment, a page of a journal, or a work of art.

Turning that sheet of paper into a work of art is really cool when your child paints with paint that he has made himself.

To make a batch of watercolor paints right in your own kitchen, you'll need:

1 tbsp. white vinegar

2 tbsp. baking soda

1 tbsp. cornstarch

1/4 tbsp. glycerin

Styrofoam egg carton

Food coloring (red, yellow, and blue)
A small mixing bowl

1. Mix the vinegar and baking soda together in a small bowl. Allow the mixture to stop foaming.

2. Add cornstarch and glycerin, mixing well.

3. Pour some mixture into the separate cups of the egg carton.

4. Add several drops of different food coloring to each carton cup. Stir until the color is well mixed. Be sure to add plenty of coloring; the color will lighten as it dries.

5. Mix the primary colors to make secondary colors.

6. For more intense colors, add powdered drink mix to the colors.

7. Let the egg carton stand overnight so the paints can harden.

97

Winter Warmers

The first snowfall of the season is a magical thing as it falls from the sky, sparkling like tiny diamonds. As soon as those flakes start, most kids are off and running to dig out their new winter wear. Make that winter wear a bit more special with some hand-decorated mittens. Even in areas with no snow, it often gets cold enough in the evening to warrant mittens, especially for little ones.

To decorate a pair of these special hand-warmers, you'll need:

Fleece or knit mittens

Cookie cutters

Cardboard or plastic quilting template

Scraps of fleece and felt

Fabric glue

Flat buttons

Small beads

Embroidery floss or pearl cotton, and a needle

Clear nail polish

Spray glitter

Yarn and crochet hook (optional)

1. Cut one large shape from the fleece or felt scraps for each mitten. Try hearts, stars, suns, stop signs, daisies, ice cream cones, or teddy bears. Cookie cutters make great patterns, too.

2. Apply a thin, even layer of glue to the back of each shape.

3. Allow the glue to dry slightly, so that it's tacky, and gently press the shapes in place paying careful attention to the edges.

4. Use embroidery floss to blanket stitch around the outside of the shapes. This will help to keep them in place and adds an extra decorative touch.

5. Sew on buttons and beads.

6. Secure any knots with a dab of clear nail polish.

7. For younger mitten wearers, crochet a length of chain stitches and securely sew an end to each mitten.

When you and your child are finished decorating the mittens, you can use an extra piece of fleece to make a matching neck warmer. Just cut a strip of fleece long enough for a scarf. Decorate the scarf as you did the mittens by gluing on shapes and sewing on buttons and beads.

And Try Some Cocoa, Too...

A winter afternoon outing—with or without snow—is made more enjoyable with a big, steaming mug of hot cocoa. In a heavy saucepan, mix together 2 tablespoons cocoa powder, 2 tablespoons white sugar, and 2 tablespoons light brown sugar. Stir in 2 cups milk. Cook over medium heat, whisking constantly until smooth and warm. Pour into two mugs. Stir a tablespoon of liquid creamer or half and half into each mug. Top with marshmallows or whipped cream.

Stay cool!

While sipping your hot cocoa, share with your child one of the many versions of *The Mitten*, a classic folktale of a menagerie of animals who make their home in a lost mitten.

98

Woolly Balls

For anyone who has ever accidentally thrown a favorite wool sweater in the washer and dryer, it's probably hard to believe that anyone would do it on purpose. But fiber artists do it all the time! It's called "felting," and it's the process of shrinking wool and other animal-based fibers to create a very heavy, dense material. Fiber artists use the process in different ways to help them create their works of art.

Using a washing machine and some brightly-dyed fiber that looks a lot like cotton candy, you and your kids can create unique, durable toys. Your best bet for locating the supplies that you'll need for this project is a spinner who might have extra or leftover fiber to sell. A locally-owned yarn shop might be able to put you in touch with a spinner.

To make some woolly balls in your own washing machine, you'll need:

Unspun wool fiber, washed and carded (sometimes called roving), natural and dyed

Small, hollow plastic balls, with or without holes
Knee-high nylons
Ivory liquid dish detergent

1. Remove any hay or other debris from the fiber that may have been missed during processing, and pull apart any large clumps of wool. Separate the fibers until you have wispy strands to work with.

2. Wrap the wool around the plastic ball. Continue wrapping until the ball is somewhat larger than you would like it to be after it's felted.

3. Use the colored fiber to build the outer layer of the ball.

4. Tuck the ball into the toe of a pair of nylons, and secure the nylon with a knot tied close to the ball. Cut the top of the nylon, leaving a 2- to 3-inch tail.

5. Put the ball through a hot wash and cold rinse in a top-loading washing machine. Add any other balls you've begun plus a few squirts of dish soap and several large, old towels for additional agitation. Be aware that the dye used to color wool may run (especially darker colors).

6. Check the ball(s) when the cycle is complete. A woolly ball should be firm, and the fibers should be fused. If there are

loose strands of wool on the outer layer, or the ball is soft, run it through another hot wash/cold rinse cycle.

7. Remove the woolly ball from the nylon.

8. Woolly balls can be put into the dryer or air dried.

Stay cool!

Make three woolly balls approximately the same size and learn to juggle!

99

Your Childhood Favorites

Most children know that at some point, Mom and Dad were children, but they usually picture their parents as smaller versions of the people they are now. It's hard for kids to believe that their parents had a favorite childhood book, toy, or type of candy. Share some of the magical moments of your childhood with your own child.

Favorite Book

Did you have a favorite childhood book that you read over and over, or a series in which you were so engrossed that you stayed up late at night, reading under the covers with a flashlight? Any book that was that special to you definitely should be shared with your child. Read a chapter out loud together for a few minutes each night before your child goes to bed.

Favorite Television Show

You probably had a favorite television show as a child. Many of the popular programs from the 1950s and 1960s are being shown on TV Land and Nick at Nite. Check for schedule information and record your childhood favorites. Share them with your child over a big bowl of popcorn.

Favorite Toy

What toys and games kept you occupied for hours at time? Maybe it was marbles, Tinker Toys, Lincoln Logs, Barbie dolls, a yo-yo, a pogo stick, a Slinky, Spirograph, or Etch a Sketch. Most of these items are still readily available today, which makes it easy to share them with your child. And while these tend to be far less sophisticated than modern electronic playthings, that's part of what makes them so cool. A toy that isn't battery-dependent can occupy your child for hours. If your favorite toy was something more obscure, you might be able to pick one up at a garage sale or from an online auction site.

Favorite Candy

Finding your favorite childhood candy might be easier than finding a rare childhood toy. If it's still made, you can purchase your former favorite from The California Candy Company. Check out their old-fashioned, hard-to-find candies at www.californiacandy.com/old-fashpage.html. (With luck, your favorite didn't make it onto the "discontinued" page. Check out the candy graveyard at www.californiacandy.com/disccandy.html.) Order a few of your childhood favorites and share them with your child while you watch *Willy Wonka & the Chocolate Factory.*

Stay cool!
Start collecting classic children's toys with your child.

100

Your *Child's* Memories

Probably the most obvious way to keep the memories alive is with photos and video. With these, you'll have visual reminders of the magical moments you and your child have shared.

Let your child take photos too. Buy an inexpensive camera for your child and let her take photos while you're doing things together. (One-time-use cameras are a good choice. With her own photos, your child will be able to capture *her* memories, which may not be exactly the same as yours.)

Protect your photographic memories by storing them properly, using archival-quality supplies. A fun way to keep your memories alive is to use the photographs to create scrapbooks. The key to a long-lasting scrapbook is in the supplies. Use only acid-free materials: paper, stickers, pens, glues and adhesives. That way, not only will your memories survive for a lifetime, you'll be able to pass them on to your children's children.

Stay cool!

Check out this book from the library: *Making Memories: A Parent's Guide to Making Childhood Memories That Last a Lifetime* by Josie Bissett.

101
Together Time

Some of your child's happiest memories are made when you and your child are simply spending time together. Enjoy their brief time in youth together.

Visit the library **together** and check out a few joke books. Try to crack each other up.

Break open a brand-new box of crayons and color **together**.

Have a pajama party **together**. Collect favorite movies, comic books, snacks, and crafts and camp out in the living room for a night, sleeping on the floor.

Plant, weed, and harvest a garden **together**.

Play with play dough **together**.

Wish on a shooting star **together**.

Build a bird feeder **together**.

Sing loudly and off-key **together**.

Do a crossword puzzle or word search **together**.

Bake a cake and lick the frosting bowl **together**.

Volunteer **together**.

Start a collection **together**.

Catch fireflies **together** (be sure to release them).

Learn something new **together**.

Watch a sunset **together**.

Run errands **together**.

Have lunch **together**.

Share a hobby or craft **together**.

Eat cookies before dinner **together**.

Lie in the grass and look for shapes in the clouds **together**.

Cook dinner **together**.

Read a classic book aloud **together**.

Stomp in rain puddles **together**.

Wash the dishes **together**.

Work on a jigsaw puzzle **together**.

Walk the dog **together** (if you don't have one, borrow the neighbor's).

Laugh **together** (often).

About the Authors

Alecia Devantier is a former educator with a master's degree in teaching, and the author of *101 Things Every Kid Should Do Growing Up*. She has written widely about family issues, educational topics, and crafts, and was a contributing writer for *HomeWords* magazine and webzine. Devantier and her husband Robert are cool parents of their three children at their home in Mt. Pleasant, Michigan.

Coauthor **Carol Turkington** is a journalist and author of countless magazine articles and more than fifty nonfiction books, specializing in parenting, education, and children's issues. Turkington, her husband Michael Kennedy, and daughter Kara spend their magical moments with two dogs, two cats, and a rabbit in Cymru, Pennsylvania.